LESSONS LEARNED
TIME
MANAGEMENT
for Success

Written by Steve Hammond

Edited by Moné Moore

Mentor Military—Lessons Learned— Time Management for Success

Printed in USA by Mentor Enterprises Inc.

PUBLISHED BY
MENTOR®
ENTERPRISES, INC.

123 Castle Dr. STE C, Madison, AL 35758

256.830.8282

admin@mentorinc.us

1st Edition, 3rd Printing

1st Edition, 2nd Printing

1st Edition, 1st Printing

ISBN-13: 978-1-940370-18-7

The views expressed in this book are those of the author and do not reflect the official policy or position of the United States Army, Defense Department, or the United States Government.

Contents

Updates and Corrections are available online at:

http://www.asktop.net/tm1ed

Access Code: HAMMTM18

FOREWORD

Time management (TM) is my hobby. Actually, at first, it was a survival tactic. Only after significant learning and success did I begin to view TM as a hobby.

I usually had control of my own schedule. There were a few jobs where I was required to punch a clock or had scheduled supervision. Keeping track of appointments, tasks, and goals made the difference between success and failure. More importantly TM reduced my frustration.

My foray into TM techniques spans nearly four decades. It doesn't take a historian to realize four decades pre-dates the desktop computer. In fact, all I really had was a clock and calendar. TM techniques have come a long way since I started figuring out how to control, or at least attempt to control, the daily requirements before me.

More productivity is expected of us today. You can't shop at a mall, eat out or drive without seeing folks connected to the cyber world. Documents that used to take a week to deliver arrive virtually instantaneously today.

I have gleaned most of the ideas in this book from others. Although the concepts have often been tweaked and personalized, I must confess to building upon foundations laid by others. There is nothing new under the sun.

When I can identify the original source, I've tried very hard to give credit where credit is due. In many instances, several sources have blended and blurred over the years so that I can no longer identify (or remember) the source to give proper credit. To those anonymous donors I offer an apology.

Early experimentation required getting a handle on whether to separate or combine personal and professional life. Along came methods for prioritizing. Then I realized that time-management needed a companion of office organization.

I started out to write only traditional management tips and tricks. I realized that organizing our workspace needed to be included. Today's business often requires travel.

I see all of these as a system. i.e. I don't really see success in personal management until all aspects have been addressed.

That being said, I do understand a modular approach that allows each person to work on one aspect at a time and not feel as though everything must be learned and changed all at once. Instead, I'm trying to ease my readers into better personal management with as many tips and tricks as I can.

I hope you enjoy this and feel it makes the difference in your life you seek.

INTRODUCTION

Psychologists tell us that there are basically two types of personalities which they simply label Type A and Type B. Type A personalities are very event-driven and are the most likely to read this book. Task oriented personalities really thrive on efficiency and better personal management.

The other personality, called Type B, is very people-oriented and gets very frustrated over discussions of how to get more things done. They go about life relying on connections to people. To them, activities and to-do's take a back seat to relationships. Type B's focus on connecting with people rather than a list is how they get things done.

If you are a Type B, perhaps the most helpful part of this book is going to be the discussion of roles and how to organize your life around the groups to which you belong. You are not likely to enjoy recording what you do and planning out details of what needs to be done.

How will you read this book?

Some of you will take a start to finish approach to this book. You will read each section and chapter sequentially just as you might read a novel.

Others may simply pick the sections and chapters that represent your greatest perceived need.

This book is written to accommodate both approaches. However, remember this. The whole concept of this book is that they work together to form one system.

Study an airplane by beginning with the wings, followed by the tail before looking in the cockpit. Just know that the plane doesn't fly without all of systems functioning together as a unit. That's the idea of this book.

My goal

My goal in laying out this book is two-fold.

One, I wish to keep the stories and illustrations to a minimum so as to show my appreciation for your time. It seems ludicrous to me to write a book about personal (time) management by deliberately making it take longer than necessary to read it. More than ludicrous, it is hypocritical.

My second goal in writing this book is to try to make each chapter like a module that could help someone reading only that chapter. My purpose here is to make this something of a reference manual that can be useful later on an idea by idea basis.

Therefore, I have attempted to make each chapter a self-contained module. The real benefit comes when combining all the modules.

In other words, if someone wanted to refresh their memory on a subject or technique they would not have to reread several chapters to get what they need. How well I have accomplished these two things remain to be seen. As long as you understand my intent, "On your mark, get set, ..."

Wait!

I want you to get the most out of this book. That means pausing as you read this book to do an exercise which will put the principle into practice.

Right now, I want you to get a pad of paper to write on as you read this book. When an exercise calls for you to do something, don't just keep reading and think you'll get it all done later. Do it right then.

Right now, I want you to write in a sentence or three why you are pursuing better TM. Prepare a list declaring what you will do with your recovered time.

Go ahead. I'll wait right here.

1

CHAOS TO ORDER

I think it is fair to say that all of us have to deal with chaos. How we choose to do so determines the outward look of our lives. Either we fail at grappling with chaos and project an image of being harried and out of control (high chaos and stress) or we do a better job of organizing the chaos and turning our lives more toward order (low chaos and stress). Just understand everyone has to deal with chaos. No one is immune.

Our individual worlds are constantly getting interrupted with items that come under the category of "miscellaneous." What to do with such stuff? We have appointments, to-dos, daily and weekly duties, short-term goals, long-term goals, bucket lists, etc.

Each of us chooses a system by which to organize our "stuff" and keep some semblance of sanity. Some of us are more comfortable with higher levels of chaos and choose to let loose organization be our approach, albeit for many this is nothing more than a smokescreen in a surrender to the life battle of being organized. Others are more meticulous and require a higher degree of organization in order to face life without the need of a strait jacket. These folks generally display a less disheveled approach to life. (But let's face it, sometimes an organized life looks boring.)

Adrenaline junkies justify the stress of less organization simply because the adrenaline rush of less control appeals more than the calmness of making order out of your world. If justifications such as, "I'm just late by nature," or "time moves faster when I am under the pressure," then this book is not for you.

Trust me, the best organized among us still have stressors such as deadlines and unmet goals. Being organized is not going to prevent the battle. It is merely an attempt to get on the winning side of a never-ending battle and cease to make excuses. If justifications leave you feeling frustrated and you aren't willing to cede the battle to chaos, then this book is for you.

Time management (TM) has been around since the industrial revolution—probably since the first humans walked the earth. The concepts have not significantly changed, though the technology has, and the methods are more refined.

Let's look at Major League Baseball. MLB has taken on more of an analytical approach, but is still essentially the same game. The purpose of this book is to cover techniques from rookie to veteran. You may already be familiar with some of the techniques and procedures we will discuss.

My goal is to make sure no one gets left behind, not even the rookies among us. It's a tall order but I build on the work of many before me. My forte is to break the battle into manage-able steps.

If I succeed, you will gain a game plan that is clear and easy to follow. This should reduce your stress level. More importantly, you should experience fewer missed deadlines and goals. This alone should feel like success.

Let's get started with an assignment. Get a pad of paper and list what you see as the biggest drawbacks your organization and productivity.

- Would your list include too many places where orga-nizational information is stored?

- Do you lack one centralized place where appointments and tasks can be recorded and retrieved?

- Is it messiness and clutter?

- Are you drowning in unfiled papers?

- Are distractions from your work causing you to take longer to get work done?

    ○ If so, what are those distractions?

- Do you have control over any of them?

- Do you allow your phone to distract you with "alerts" that you have messages, social media posts, email, etc.?

- Do you know how to turn those off via your phone settings?

This book will help you with these types of issues.

WHY ARE YOU READING THIS BOOK?

You need to establish something right out of the gate.

- What is the real goal of TM?
  - The obvious answer to this question is to achieve greater efficiency. But you must ask the next question.

- Why are you interested in being more efficient?
  - Again, the obvious answer is to have more free time.

- If you had more free time, what would you do with it?

- Would you spend more time with your family?

- Would you spend more time at the beach? Fishing?

- Would you spend more time at work trying to get even more done?

- Would it be to earn more money?
  - Why? To live a life of luxury? To retire earlier?

By answering these follow-up questions, you will find your true motivation for TM. What is it you would do with that extra time the efficiency gives you?

Perhaps you're thinking you need a little more productivity. Why?

- Perhaps you want to move to the next level financially

- Get work done sooner so you don't have to take anything home

- Stop using your "day off" to catch up;

- Be able to take up a hobby

- Pursue your passion

- Rebuild your marriage relationship

- Establish a better connection with the kids

For most, I suspect the answer is some combination of the above.

What bothers me is a person pursuing TM and efficiency without a clear reason why. **Dogs chase their tails. Humans should not.**

Upon further reflection, perhaps the answer to the question about why would you pursue better management of time, is so you might achieve a better balance of multiple priorities in your life. Every area of your life is clamoring for more attention and more time. When you allow one area of your life to dominate others, life becomes a washing machine in spin cycle and the clothes have become unbalanced and the washer is bouncing across the floor. Life begins to jump around and act chaotically. Sometimes you just need to pause the machine (life) long enough to spread the clothes around (time allocation) and restart the machine.

If you do not have a clear reason for reading this book, it is likely you will gather some ideas, but change nothing in your life.

I think it is time you pause reading just long enough to think this through.

On your pad of paper, work through the reason(s) for pursuing TM. Don't just keep it in your head. It won't be clearly worked out up there. Forcing your thoughts into sentences clears the fog and makes the ideas more specific.

Jot down one to three bullet points on what you intend to do with recovered time.

SUMMARY POINTS

- Are you serious about Time Management and implementing these strategies?

- Are you willing to consolidate all places of record into one place?

- Why are you reading this book? Write the reasons down on a piece of paper.

2

GROUND RULES

In baseball, the managers meet with the umpires before the game to go over the rules. I think it prudent we begin by naming three principles behind the rest of the book.

1.   We don't manage time, we manage ourselves.

Personal discipline does not come easy for most of us. Part of the problem is we want instant success—just push a button or add water and stir. Discipline is really the long-term effect of making daily, and moment-by-moment, choices that develop into habits. These habits form the basis of genuine discipline.

Trying to establish instant discipline is like trying to become a weight lifter by beginning with weights twice your body weight. If we are going to become disciplined in the area of TM, we are going to have to focus on the daily choices which develop discipline. Think of it like forging a chain link by link.

You don't make a chain all at once. If you make links and join them together, you get a chain. You don't get a habit by deciding to have a habit. You form that habit chain one link at a time.

Whenever someone uses the excuse, "I didn't have time," I remind myself that we all have the same amount of time. The question is how we use time.

Therefore, I don't like to use the term TM, although it is a common phrase. I prefer to use the term **personal management** to remind myself it is not time we manage, but ourselves against time. How we choose to use time is the key.

Now to be fair, what some might mean is, "I didn't have enough time over which I had control." Too much time went to what others control. I get that.

Be sure of this, TM, personal management, whatever you choose to call it, is a control issue. We need to be in charge or the whole matter is pointless.

WHY IS TIME MANAGEMENT IMPORTANT?

Let me clarify my point clearer. Most of us have heard advertisements about investment seminars. Some of us have attended them. Perhaps you have heard the adage, "Real estate is your biggest investment." I would like to challenge the concept. I would suggest your biggest investment in life is in how you use your time. I've seen people make mistakes in real estate or the stock market and earn back more money later. I've never seen anyone recover time, although I do admit I've seen poor TM turned into an advantage by using **lessons learned**.

When it comes to TM, "killing time" or "wasting time" should be seen in the same way lighting cigars with hundred-dollar bills would be seen. Trading something as valuable as time for something of lesser value is something to avoid.

Many people at the end of their life do not have enough money to be independent. When asked why, the most common excuse is, "I had too many bills and obligations and couldn't afford to invest."

But anyone skilled in investment strategies will tell you that the successful investor **makes** the effort and uses whatever they can. They make sacrifices on short-term goals to fund long term-goals. They learn how to invest *small amounts* rather than waiting for the *big chunk*.

> Time is a form of investment. In fact, it is the only one for which you cannot recover what is lost.

Start with whatever time you can control. Don't sweat the part that others control. There may come a day when more of your time is under your control. Then you can see greater rewards. For now, start with what you can control.

Next, *memory is the weakest link in any system*. Did you know many experts estimate those who work from lists accomplish 30% more than those who just utilize memory and thinking? *That means I want to use my memory as little as possible* when it comes to what I need to accomplish and where I need to be. Therefore, I want the absolute minimum time between when I think a thought and when I record the thought. This keeps my memory out of the system as much as possible.

Going back to the analogy of the chain, my memory is the weakest link. The chain can be no stronger than my ability to *remember* every detail of where I need to be and what I need to accomplish. The downside to this approach is that I must use an inordinate amount of mental power trying to remember. This is because our ability to remember details is dependent upon how deeply ingrained those details are in our memory.

Neuroscientists tell us that moving something from the short-term memory to a longer-term memory is somehow connected to the number of times we have encountered that detail.

Thinking of something you need to do next week, and believing you will still remember it next week after encountering the thought only once, is folly. The reality is that if you remember it next week it is because you have rehearsed it over and over in your mind. The *hit* on your mental power is beyond necessary.

The effective time manager seeks to reduce the amount of time the memory is involved in any activity or appointment. Removing the memory entirely is out of the question. The goal is to have the least amount of time between thinking a thought and recording it in a TM system that replaces the memory.

Consider the following story told about Albert Einstein. With an IQ of 140, we now know that Albert Einstein had something currently known as dyslexia. In Einstein's day, they did not have a name for this or a diagnosis.

To oversimplify an explanation of dyslexia, let me refer to it as being able to grasp "big picture" items, but not being able to sort out details. Chances are, if you had actually known and worked around Albert Einstein, you probably would have a very different view of him then is the current mythology. Rumors abound about his struggles with everyday details. One is that he needed two different routes for walking to Princeton and home because he couldn't remember which one was his destination. Only by using two different routes was he able to distinguish which destination was his goal.

In another example, he would approach students on campus and say to them, "My name is Albert Einstein. Do you know where I live, and would you show me the way home?" Even though he had walked there many times, he struggled with keeping track of the route and location.

It is said that his wife wound up painting their front door red so that it would help him spot the house and not walk right by it, as he had apparently done numerous times.

Is this the mental picture you had of Einstein? Likely not.

A colleague of his recognized this as an unnamed problem. The colleague simply said, "Al, do you even know your own address?" With that very pronounced accent of his, Einstein said, "Absolutely, I know my own address." "Then prove it." the colleague replied. According to the account,

Einstein proceeded over to a shelf, found a phonebook (remember there were no smartphones or internet), picked it up, looked up his own name, and read the man his own address out of the phone book. "I knew you didn't know your address!" The colleague said.

Whereupon Einstein replied, "I do know my own address. I just make it a habit not to remember anything I can look up!"

And there you have one of the great secrets of preserving the mind for more important matters. Never waste brainpower on something that could be recorded, including keeping track of where you have to be and what you have to do. This was Einstein's method for preserving his brain for the weightier matters for which he is known.

The legend of Albert Einstein wouldn't exist if he had used up his mental power remembering trivial details.

This is where learning to use a recorded system will take you to accomplishment levels you cannot imagine. Then, you can either get more done, or kick back for something not measured in to-do's.

If you are not using a list/calendar method of attacking duties, chores and responsibilities, it is likely because you have not found a convenient tool/system that is accessible at all times. Hopefully, that is about to change.

Any system that is going to both increase your efficiency and relieve your stress over the load you carry, must reduce the amount of brain power being used.

The more we use our brains, the more we stress ourselves over not forgetting something important.

Memory is one of the worst uses of our brain. Storage of information is not one of the brains better functions.

I know that the current stereotype is the smart person is the person that has everything stored in their memory. This common myth is that the ability to access information in the brain's memory in any given situation is what qualifies them as smart. It probably only qualifies them as overly stressed.

Besides, neuroscientists tell us the brain rests certain sectors at various times, preventing the brain from shutting down from fatigue. In other words, the brain cannot entirely shut down or we wouldn't be able to live, much less function. We're not C-3PO. So, the brain accomplishes its rest in small amounts at a time.

This explains why sometimes we cannot remember something right now, but a few minutes later it "comes back to us." If the information we are trying to remember happens to be stored in a part of the brain currently at rest.

Additionally, the way someone remembers something is to go over and over and over the item. This uses a tremendous amount of brain power just to get it stored.

Consider this:

- have you ever had an important thought in the middle of the night, but decided to "remember it" rather than writing it down somewhere?

- What happened the next day?

    ◦ Not only could you not remember the thought, you couldn't remember the subject or context.

This is proof that it takes a lot of brain power to rehearse and rehearse what you are trying to remember.

- Have you ever felt like your "photographic memory" was lacking film?

- How do you remember an appointment or a set of numbers?

    ◦ You keep reminding yourself of it in hopes of not forgetting.

Think of the brain like a battery that stores a charge. Using that battery when it is not necessary reduces its capacity to provide a charge when it is called upon.

When I was a young boy, my Father used to keep a flashlight for emergencies such as the power going out or needing to relight a furnace. It seemed each time there was an emergency, the batteries in the flashlight had been drained. Now I don't know who would have used their Father's emergency flashlight for frivolous reasons, but I can tell you that the tents we used to make by putting blankets over chairs could very dark without some kind of light. It wasn't my fault.

Trying to use the brain to keep track of appointments and "to-do's" reduces the brain's ability to perform more important functions like creative thinking.

So, the second principle is to not use your brain as your database, or at least use it as little as possible when remembering where you have to be and what you have to do...

The third principle is that it is always **easier to fire the retros** on a rocket already in space than it is to build a new rocket and try to launch it into space.

This reminds me that tweaking an existing system is easier than creating a new one. Some of you are hoping for an entirely new system a.k.a. *a silver bullet*. I'm guessing that for most of you firing a retro in the system you already have will get your rocket ship back on course.

Most of us have some contrivance of a tool for organizing ourselves. It might be anything from a spiral notebook to note cards to a sophisticated computer program to an app on our smart phone.

What you should be looking for is enhancing your system by using baby steps rather than seeking an entirely new system. Add a few steps to the dance you already know rather than going for an entirely new dance.

To be sure, some of you reading this either have no structure in place or one that is so ineffective, it should be replaced.

At the end of the day, what we need is a system that is *convenient* and *accessible*. Convenient means it must be easy to get information into and out of. Overly complicated or bulky organizers do not work. Accessible means the organizer must also be readily at hand no matter where we are when we need to put information in or get some out—with us at all times (OK, maybe not in the shower, or in our uniform back pocket while on the ball diamond, but just close by.).

CAN WE REALLY CONTROL OUR TIME?

Let's be very clear about something. We all have 24 hours in a day, and seven days in a week. The Beatles might try to bolster their promise of love, but they cannot get "eight days a week" any more than someone can give 110% of their effort. The position of the sun and the earth's rotation are fixed.

As I said before, I don't really like the phrase *TM*. Since time is fixed, I wish the common phrase were more along the lines of self-management. The concept of TM needs to be understood, not as getting more time, but by a more efficient use of the time we have been given, i.e. the management of a fixed amount of time, not the creation of more time.

HOW DO WE RELATE TO TIME?

One of the first self-assessment exercises that I recommend is to ascertain just how much the concept of time interacts with your thinking. Some people, by nature or by training, are very attuned to the passage of time.

On a few occasions, I've had the opportunity to sit behind a radio microphone. It doesn't take long to realize the importance of timing a song's introduction so that you do not "step on" the lyrics of the song. I've also done small amount of hosting a radio talk show. Knowing how to close off a discussion without crossing the "hard break" at the top of the hour for news or a commercial demands keen sense of what can or cannot be said in 10 seconds.

On the other hand, I am sure you have experienced times of recreation, pleasure or excitement where you "lost track of all time." Experiencing a breakthrough in solving a problem, shopping while a spouse waits and coming to dinner right after conquering the next level of the game come to mind as examples of having more time pass than we realize.

As we explore the concept of managing ourselves against time throughout this book, please keep these three principles in mind:

1. We manage ourselves more than time

2. Our memory is a poor tool for managing much of anything, don't even try it with time

3. If you can tweak a system you are already familiar and comfortable with, don't scrap it for something new. This does not apply if what you're doing is utterly failing.

In the next chapter, we are going to take a look at something that most books on this subject fail to address.

Have you ever asked yourself the question, "When am I good?" Well, I'm about to show you why you should.

EXERCISE

1. Think about what you got done yesterday. How about the entire week?

2. Ask yourself how much of your accomplishments are coming from "remembering" you have to do them. How many are from a working list? Where is that list? Or are you just trying to remember what you did?

3. Start thinking about a different way to handle these items. What are your options?

4. Pick out at least 3 possible ways you think might work for you. Don't try to choose just one yet.

SUMMARY

1. We manage ourselves more than time

2. Time is the most important investment and any loss is unrecoverable.

3. Our memory is a poor tool for managing much of anything, don't even try it with time

4. Start with what you can control instead of using what you can't control as a barrier to action.

5. If you can tweak a system you are already familiar and comfortable with, don't scrap it for something new. This does not apply if what you're doing is utterly failing.

3

USING ROUTINES

Everyone, and I mean everyone, has a list of items that must be done repeatedly. Some of these items are repeated daily or weekly, some are repeated on other schedules, but we all have things we must do over and over.

Most people do not think intentionally about these lists. Mornings are harried because *remembering* what needs to be done is the typical SOP (standard operating procedure).

The efficient user of time thinks intentionally about these routines rather than randomly waiting until the brain remembers the next action. Checklists replace the memory. These lists are adjusted as changes are required, but checklists beat memory ever time.[1]

Talk to a successful, productive person about their routines and you'll likely find someone who can produce a list of exactly what they do repeatedly, when and in what order. This is not a coincidence.

---

1   Recommended reading: The Checklist Manifesto, How To Get Things Right, by Atul Gawande

Good time managers make good use of routines. Routines reduce the amount of brain power required to do those actions that must happen on a regular basis and shouldn't require brain drain. These routines reduce the number of decisions we have to make. They reduce the stress on the memory as well as the inevitable missteps from forgetting one or more actions (Ever walk out the door and remember something you meant to do, but forgot?). Even more importantly, they increase our efficiency.

You have probably laughed about a scene in a movie where someone opens the closet and has a series of suits which are all identical. In fact, there are many reasons why the military, some schools, and certain businesses require uniforms. This is not only for identification purposes. It also reduces the number of choices a person has to make (there are other reasons as well).

Choosing what clothes to wear each morning is actually a routine. Failure to recognize this as a routine requires additional time, stress over choices, and a lack of predictability to this daily routine. While some value the emotional choice of deciding what to wear according to what they *feel* like wearing at that particular moment, honesty would require that they also admit the additional time to choose and some stress associated with the choice.

But choosing our clothing is just one small part of a morning routine. What about other parts of your life that have a repetitive nature?

THREE POSSIBLE *DAILY* ROUTINES

Let's start with the **morning routine**. I want you to take a moment and jot down what you have to do every single morning, or at least what you have to do every single workday morning.

- Do you have to shave?

- Put on makeup?

- Shower?

- Toiletries?

- What other grooming habits do you repeat?

- Do you eat breakfast?

- Brush/floss teeth?

- Take vitamins or medications?

- Have you ever started to put on some clothing only to find out it has already been worn and isn't clean?

- Do you have responsibility for anyone else?

- Do you have a quiet time for long-range thinking, reading, meditating or praying?

- Do you need to check email, social media, weather or a news source (email and news in the morning can be very distracting from *your* plan—try to avoid it until later[2])?

---

2   Read <u>Never Check eMail in the Morning</u>, by Julie Morgenstern.

- Do you need to look over your daily plan to see if there's anything you need to check or do or anyone you need to contact?

These are just a few of the items that might be a part of a daily morning routine.

Thinking intentionally about this morning routine will allow you to establish the best way to go about it with the least amount of skipped or forgotten items. Admittedly, one might summarize things to be done in the bathroom by just saying *grooming* or *personal prep* or *hygiene.* This might be sufficient. It depends on how much brain power you use to remember each activity. But knowing how much time this requires is essential.

I once consulted for someone who was struggling to get to work on time. I started asking what items needed to be performed each morning. Then I asked how long each item took. My final question was what time this person rose each morning. What I found was that the person was rising one and a half hours prior to needing to leave and trying to accomplish 2 ½ hours of morning routine. You don't have to be a math major to see why this person was consistently late. They had not thought intentionally about their morning routine. They just felt that an hour and a half should be sufficient. If you would like to leave for work with a slower pace, try planning a morning routine that allows a few minutes to do nothing prior to leaving. You might find it a very valuable addition to your morning routine.

Now let's take a moment and think about an **evening routine**. This is harder for many people because many do not think they do the same thing each evening. They are probably correct in one sense, but they are incorrect if they do not think there are some things that they do repeatedly.

Take a moment and jot down anything you do prior to retiring from the day, as well as anything you wish you would do before retiring from the day. This might include:

- Brush/floss teeth

- Dress for sleep,

- Turn the covers back

- Drink water

- Take medication(s)

- Journal

- Focus on something inspirational

- Clear any negative emotions

- Verbalize love to family members

- Tuck children in/read to them

- Look over tomorrow's plan

- Adjust thermostat

- Set alarm (I very much object to awakening to something called an "alarm"), etc.

Most people do these things from rote memory and fail to see them as a list. They have done no intentional thinking about what is done each evening, let alone what would be desirable to do. Consequently, some things get missed and some remain elusive wishes that don't happen.

Ever had to get out of bed to do something that you do every night, but tonight you forgot? Thinking intentionally about an evening routine can simplify the process.

Now let's consider thinking about an **end of work routine**. This one is a little more nuanced as the tendency of work becoming more mental causes the lines between work and home to blur. If, however, you work at a location that is different from your residence, it would be good to set up an end of work routine. Even if you work at home, I recommend a special space in the house for "work" that is separate from personal/family living. The reason I recommend this is the number one complaint among Fortune 500 companies is that people bring home problems to work and take work problems home.

Nick Sabin and Tom Coughlin are just two of the coaches that have counseled their players to *be where your feet are*. This, of course, is encouraging players to forget off-field distractions or the failure of the last play. It is attempting to teach them that the play going on **now** is the one that matters.

In the work-a-day world this means not allowing your mind to be somewhere besides where it should be. If you are at home concentrate on home. If you're at work concentrate on work, etc. This seems so simple, and yet many people struggle with this. It wouldn't be the number one complaint of business owners otherwise.

Here is a psychological technique for being where your feet are. Create a routine that sets up a mental and emotional break that separates one place from another.

Someone once shared a story with me about a fellow who developed a rather curious routine, but this routine apparently worked very well for him. According to what my friend told me, he would drive by a vacant lot that was on his way to and from work. On the way home each evening, he would pause in front of this vacant lot, reach over the backseat of his car, open the back door, and say to all of his imaginary problems from work, "All right, all of you, get out! I'll be back to pick you up in the morning." He would then proceed to close the door and finish his commute home. According to my friend, the key to making this really work for him was that on the way to work the next morning he would again stop in front of the vacant lot, open the back door of the car and say, "All right, everybody back in."

This rather bizarre story indicates the concept of creating a mental and emotional barrier that would keep us from being where our feet are. This gentleman had found that a physical act repeated each day at the end of work could keep him from bringing his work problems home with him and changing his mood and interactions with family members who weren't a part of the problem or solution.

Before we go any further, let me hasten to add, that the mind is sometimes a very unruly servant. It will drift to places where our feet aren't until we catch it. The key lies in how we deal with those drifting thoughts. If we try to remember them until we get to work, we add stress and distraction to our present location/situation. If, however, we learn how to capture that thought so that we can put it out of our mind, then we may return to where our feet are. We will explore different options on how to make quick work out of capturing these thoughts and putting them out of our mind in chapters five and six.

What routines do you do at the end of each workday, and what routines do you wish you would do at the end of every workday? Thinking intentionally about these things, listing them, and putting them into a practical order will greatly simplify the process. Why not take a moment right now and start to develop just such a list?

Now let's turn our attention to those repetitive items which are not on a daily basis.

Let's think intentionally for a moment about **weekly routines**. What items do you repeat on a weekly basis? Are there any you wish to do, but don't seem to accomplish?

At work

- Do you file?

- Write weekly reports?

- Vacuum your office?

- Water plants?

- Feed fish?

- Take something home to be cleaned?

At home, would it be household chores? For example:

- Do you do laundry/dry cleaning?

- Dusting, vacuuming?

- Mowing/gardening (seasonal)?

- Banking?

- Grocery shopping?

- Cooking the upcoming week's menu to freeze, etc.?

- Do you run kids to sports or play them yourself?

- Do you have a date night, or a guys'/girls' night out?

- Do you have church, civic clubs or other weekly meetings?

- Do you hit the gym on weekends?

- Restart a laptop, tablet or phone?

Have you ever taken the time to list these weekly repetitions and actually thought about how much time you give to each? If you will do that right now, you will find that you can make much better advanced decisions instead of using memory and last-minute choosing. I think it is very important for individuals to actually plan naps and downtime for physical recovery. I know camping, sports, parties, and a host of other activities, while enjoyable, can leave us exhausted instead of rested. Looking intentionally at what is desirable in the way of activity while acknowledging the need for physical rest can be a stress relieving exercise.

Let's next consider **monthly routines**. You have repetitive actions that need to be done on a monthly basis.

- How often do you need to pay bills?

- Do you have a schedule for clearing weeds (seasonal)?

- Do you clean refrigerator/check for items past expiration date?

- Do you maintain certain appliances/devices by cleaning filters or wiping them down?

- Do you wash, clean and de-clutter vehicles including seats, pockets and compartments?

What are your **quarterly routines?**

- Do you deep clean the whole house?

- Do you have to turn in financial reports or send quarterly tax filings?

- Change certain seasonal decorations?

- Change the oil/service vehicles?

- De-clutter drawers?

The more you think intentionally about these things, the more you move from remembering (or forgetting) and wishing to executing these routines with a less stressful plan.

Take a moment right now and start a list of those items in which seasonal/quarterly attention is required or desired. You will think of more things as time passes and your memory or desire prompts you, but *starting* the list is an important first step.

What are your **semi-annual routines**?

- Do you check/replace smoke detector batteries, defrost freezer, check HVAC filters, etc.

- Do you need to clean/organize a shed, garage or other storage space?

- Clean gutters?

- Inspect roof, driveway, alternate screens and storm windows?

- Do you own an RV that needs winterizing or preparing for the RV season?

These items need not be left to memory and mood. They can be listed and completed with calmness and composure. It only requires thinking intentionally and using a list.

When I moved away from trying to remember what I needed to do each year to using a reminder list, I put defrost the freezer on an annual routine. By the time the year rolled around the freezer had become very troublesome. I switched this to a semi-annual routine and found that it took less time in two separate chores than it did in one. I don't like defrosting the freezer. Two quick sessions is much better to me than one long one.

What about **annual routines?**

- Do you file your own taxes (perhaps including a software purchase and installation) or hire someone to prepare them (requiring an appointment and document gathering/organization)?

- Do you think/plan holiday gatherings, travel or purchases?

- Do you schedule vacation time?

- Do you have to record healthcare needs or annual enrollment changes at work?

- Consider what needs painting? Winterize the outside of house (hoses and hose bib protection), store lawn furniture, etc. What is the reverse in the springtime?

- Do you raise a flag in the warmer months then take it down in winter months?

- These could be combined in a toggle pattern for annual routines or separated and listed under semi-annual routines.

It just requires thinking, planning and setting triggers to make this work. In the long-run we use up less energy, stress and time.

WRAPPING UP ROUTINES

Finally, plan what kind of tickler file would you use as a trigger to keep you from having to remember to do these routines. Would a calendar app on your phone, a reminder app or a 3 X 5 card file with different colors for different routines be your way to get these routines done routinely? Remember this; writing it down is the easy part. Checking the list routinely is the hard part. That's why I favor a timed prompt that comes at me when I need it to. I don't want alerts that other people control and serve to distract me, but I do want alerts over which I have control to keep me doing what is important to me.

The more we have a system to prompt us the less stress we experience trying to use our faulty memory as a prompt.

FINAL QUESTION

Did you actually make any of these lists?

SUMMARY

Make checklists

Include:

- Morning routines

- Evening routines

- End of work routines

- Weekly routines

- Monthly routines

- Semi-annual routines

- Annual routines

- Shopping Routines

- Maintenance Routines

4

ENERGY; THE FORGOTTEN FORCE

Most books on TM overlook the importance of managing energy levels. No amount of planning and organization can overcome the state of your energy level. When your energy level is low at any critical moment, you are either unable to perform a given tasks or it takes longer to perform the specified task. Many people give up on TM books, plans, and planners because energy management is not taken into consideration.

GETTING IN SYNC WITH OUR CIRCADIAN RHYTHMS[1]

"What is a circadian rhythm?" It is sometimes referred to as the "body clock." It is the physiological mechanism within your body that tells you when to sleep, wake, eat, etc. and it exists in virtually all living things. Although these rhythms can be

---

1   A daily cycle of biological activity based on a 24-hour period and influenced by regular variations in the environment, such as the alternation of night and day. Circadian rhythms include sleeping and waking in animals, flower closing and opening in angiosperms, and tissue growth and differentiation in fungi. www.dictionary.com/browse/circadian-rhythm

externally affected by environmental cues such as sunlight and temperature, there is a programming on the inside of each of us that makes us prone to increased productivity at certain times and decreased productivity at others.

These circadian rhymes are at work within each of us and we constantly face situations that force us to violate them. A deadline pushes us to work though the fatigue that tells us to stop. An alarm goes off, though our body says more sleep is needed. We work through lunch even though we would like to eat

Someone who is forced to rise very early for work, but easily sleeps in on days off, is showing that rising early is not the default mode. On the other hand, if you rise early on your days off, that is a signal coming from your body clock that rising early is not affecting your sleep.

Enjoying late nights is also a cue. There are folks who can get more done after everyone else has turned in for the night,

It does absolutely no good to teach a method of TM that makes everyone experience the same rise and fall in energy levels. These are the physiological cues that can impact your performance.

How this relates to TM is that many people schedule their day without regard to their natural energy levels. Putting detailed or heavily cognitive tasks during times when the body clock is likely to be at a low energy level makes tasks more dreaded, slower to accomplish, and overall more difficult.

The result is that accomplishing less tends to discourage us from planning. This can cause a negative outlook and leave us farther behind in our work. Some just give up on planning altogether and let "what happens, happen."

TAKING OUR BIORHYTHMS INTO ACCOUNT

The best-case scenario allows us to learn how to match the task to the anticipated energy level, then allow for "mid-course corrections" to take place if our body is reacting to external stimuli.

Some individuals come to work with little sleep and still try to function according to the previously developed plan without taking into account the change in energy levels. They push through the day accomplishing much less than if they had taken into account their lowered energy level. We must learn to plan and adapt our day based on our energy levels whenever possible.

Recent books tried to capitalize on Mark Twain's advice, "Eat the ugly frog first." This approach advises getting the most dreaded task out of the way first gives one a sense of accomplishment and improves the outlook on the rest of the day.

A sense of accomplishment is a positive step in the right direction. I like the idea of having the worst part of the day done and behind me. However, is this the most productive way to attack the day? Probably not if your energy level is low at the beginning of the work day. However, the person who begins their day with high energy levels will appreciate Mark Twain's advice. This person will make great use of the concept, perhaps even touting it to others as the best approach. Individuals who are not a "morning" person will sigh and wonder what is wrong with them. Nothing is wrong with them. They just have different biorhythms.

What seems to be a much better approach is to match the "ugly frog" with our highest energy points. So, with all due respect to one of my favorite authors, Mark Twain, I would like to modify his advice to state: "Eat the ugly frog when you have ugly frog-eating energy." Just be sure you know the difference between matching your energy to the task and simply avoiding what you don't want to do. This is not meant to be a procrastination tool.

Highly cognitive work, decision-making or goal planning should not be scheduled for low-energy times. Naturally, I am not referring to appointments over which we have no control. These are called hard appointments. We have no flexibility in dealing with these types of situations. We do not control when they happen. These must be accomplished in spite of energy levels. This is the time to suck it up and "get 'er done." You may not feel as clever or as quick, but you do the best you can.

If you need to be at your best for a meeting, and you have any influence over when the meeting is to take place, try to schedule it when you are at your peak energy level. However, if you are required to attend an FYI meeting that will do little to advance your priorities, see if you can get it scheduled for when your energy level is not at its peak because odds are you would not accomplish much anyway. Our goal is to learn how to schedule those tasks requiring the most energy when we are at our peak performance level.

> One of the keys to success is learning how to turn our tasks into soft appointments. Soft appointments are more flexible, so we want to pay very close attention to our energy levels. Therefore, it is imperative we take an accurate assessment of our biological clock, and determine the high-energy and low-energy times of our day.

Most of us are familiar with the general "rooster" vs "night-owl" designations. These give us a general idea, but are much too broad to be of practical use in detailed planning.

Let's take a more serious and technical look at what actually happens in a typical day.

Most of you reading this will intuitively have a general idea of when you are "at your best." If you have absolutely no clue when you are at your best, simply spend a few days paying attention to the time of day you do your best work. Also, pay attention the time of day when you have trouble thinking through situations, making plans or decisions.

You should see a pattern from day to day. This pattern is your circadian rhythm.

HOW CIRCADIAN RHYTHMS WORK

Let's say you need to be at work by 8:00am. You arrive at work feeling sluggish and not able to think clearly. You turn on your computer, stumble to the coffee pot, pour yourself a cup of coffee, and proceed to stand there for a long period of time trying to get your senses. You're not ready to start work until the floor once again appears level. Now let's suppose that this is not due to a particularly late night or high energy expenditure from the previous day. Yesterday, last night and this morning were pretty normal. Let's further suppose that this is pretty much your pattern each day. However, you also notice that each day you tend to begin humming and turning out productive work by 8:30. Except at 9:45 it seems someone disconnected some wires inside you and the pace of your work begins to slow. Although you try stretching and eating an apple or more coffee you don't really get much accomplished until around 10:30–10:45. Then another burst of energy causes you to work productively until your lunch break. Paying attention to the afternoon you observe yourself in similar ebbs and flows. Note and log the times. After a few days, you see a pattern that your best, most productive work seems to come between 3 and 5 pm. You also notice you accomplished the second-most work from 8:30–9:30am. Your third-best time is between 10:30–and Noon. This is vital information to keep in mind when it comes to planning a schedule.

Keep in mind that holidays, home pressures and over-indulged hobbies can affect these patterns. You are trying to find the patterns that are the "default" mode, not energy mostly affected by abnormal events.

Believe it or not, there are people who wake up in high gear. They rarely sleep until the alarm clock goes off. Their mind is racing from the get-go. They are at work long before they physically arrive. These folks often prefer to arrive at work before they are scheduled to be there in order to accomplish their best work before the interruptions start. Great ideas are coming at rapid pace. Solutions to yesterday's late afternoon quandaries now seem obvious. Until it stops. At some point, it feels like someone tripped a breaker inside their head. The mind checks out for a period of time. Time to switch to something less mentally demanding.

Once these patterns are observed, they can serve as the framework for a general planning of the week. These biorhythms are an essential element in increased productivity.

This is even more important when you learn that I'm going to recommend against daily planning. A weekly plan that is only slightly altered from day to day is a more effective way of avoiding reactionary work on less important items. I'll say more about this in Chapter 10.

Now that you have a general idea of your biorhythms, you will be able to use this information to plan your most productive times and get the most critical tasks. Consequently, the least cognitive tasks are assigned to those times when you anticipate not performing at your highest level.

I can't tell you how many people I have observed who arrive at work already in high-energy-mode and begin answering email—a task which likely doesn't require a lot of RPMs and probably does more to derail their plans in favor of someone else's plans based on the contents of the email. If your high-energy times are being given to email, social media, watching/listening to the news, you are contributing to your own lack of success.

Of all the tips you get from this book, this one tip of cooperating with your own biorhythms may do the most to increase your productivity.

Spend serious time getting a handle on your high and low energy periods and use them in weekly scheduling. You'll be amazed at the increase in productivity.

Summary Points:

- Do you have an understanding of your biorhythms a.k.a. circadian rhythms?

- When do you perceive yourself having the best energy?

- Have you learned to place hard appointments in your schedule?

- Have you learned how to use soft appointments to coordinate your to-do list with your calendar so as to keep a realistic approach to responsibilities?

5

FOCUS, FOCUS, FOCUS

USING THE POMODORO APPROACH

Distractions are the bane of productivity. Whether it is a ringing phone, a coworker's question or a loud noise, we seem to live in a world of distractions that keep us from working at our most productive level.

Some try to deal with this by playing music. but this is simply one more distraction.

There are some distractions which are unavoidable. There is no point in talking about these as they are beyond your control. What I would like to address are a few of the most common distractions for which there is a fix.

THE MYTH OF MULTITASKING

If you are like most people, you are being asked to operate at an unreasonable level. The demand simply outstrips the time. One common response to this demand is an approach to work commonly referred to as a *multitasking*. Many people feel that if they work on more than one thing at a time, there is an increase in productivity. In fact, the opposite is actually true. The attempt to multi-task slows us down.

By its definition, multitasking is the accomplishing of multiple tasks simultaneously. To do this, the brain must be capable of thinking two thoughts at once.

mul·ti·task (məltētask, məltītask∕)

verb

gerund or present participle: **multitasking**

1. (of a person) deal with more than one task at the same time.

But the brain isn't actually capable of thinking two thoughts at once.

Then why do many people think they can multitask? The answer lies in the misconceptions about what multitasking really is.[1]

The first misconception people have is that they think they are doing two tasks, but only one of them actually requires

---

[1]   These Are The Long-Term Effects of Multitasking

Being constantly connected may keep you from getting fired, but making time for deep work is what will get you promoted.

https://www.fastcompany.com/3057192/these-are-the-long-term-effects-of-multitasking

Want To Be More Productive? Stop Multi-Tasking

https://www.forbes.com/sites/lisaquast/2017/02/06/want-to-be-more-productive-stop-multi-tasking/#34a23d6d55a6 thought. You might be doing two things, but one of them is purely "muscle memory." For example, someone might read their smart phone while they walk. This does not qualify as multitasking because the brain is not consciously involved in walking. Putting one foot in front of another is something we have done long enough to accomplish it without conscious thinking. If we, in fact, had to concentrate on putting one foot in front of the other, we would not be able to simultaneously read our phone.

The other misconception about multitasking is that switching between multiple tasks is the same thing as multitasking. This is the definition most often used for multitasking, but if we look at the definition of multitasking, we see that that it does not line up with our common assumption.

When we are trying to accomplish multiple tasks at one time, we do what the processor in a computer does. We alternate between tasks. We are really only doing one task at a time, even though we are alternating between multiple tasks.

Do you think you can talk on the phone and type the same time? You cannot. While you are listening, you're not actually typing. When you begin to type, you're not actually listening. The reason many people are fooled into thinking they are doing two things at once is the brains amazing ability to fill in "gaps" in a message.

If you listen to a few words someone says, then cease listening while you type a few words, then return to listening, your brain can figure out what the other person said while you were not listening. This causes many people to believe they actually did hear what the person said while typing. But if you type for a little too long, you prove you weren't really listening because you have to ask the person to repeat what they said. Your brain simply could not fill in the gap.

Are you one of those people who believe that they can text while safely driving? Hopefully you now realize what you are really doing is jumping back and forth between concentrating on driving and concentrating on your phone. If you sit in your car and merely stare at the shape of the phone, your peripheral vision can see outside the cockpit. But as soon as you actually begin to read text, your focus closes down and you cannot see outside the cockpit. This is not only dangerous for you, but for those who are on the road near you.

Studies have proven that this "jump-back-and-forth" approach is actually slower and less productive. Nancy K. Napier, PhD, writing in a blog for *Psychology Today*[2] refers to an exercise which proves switching between tasks takes longer. She writes:

> *Take a small test that I learned recently in a workshop about mindfulness, delivered by the Potential Project, a group based out of Denmark. Here's the test:*
> *Draw two horizontal lines on a piece of paper*
> *Now, have someone time you as you carry out the two tasks that follow:*

2   Nancy K. Napier Ph.D. https://www.psychologytoday.com/blog/creativity-without-borders/201405/the-myth-multitasking

On the first line, write:

I am a great multitasker

On the second line: write out the numbers 1-20 sequentially,
like those below:

1 2 3 4 5 6 7 8 9 10 11 12 13 14 15 16 17 18 19 20

How much time did it take to do the two tasks? Usually
it's about 20 seconds.

Now, let's multitask.

Draw two more horizontal lines and have someone time
you. Write a letter on one line, and then a number on the
line below, then the next letter in the sentence on the upper
line, and then the next number in the sequence, changing
from line to line. In other words, you write the letter "I" and
then the number "1" and then the letter "a" and then the
number "2" and so on, until you complete both lines.

I'll bet you your time is double or more your previous time.
You also may have made errors and you were probably
frustrated since you had to "rethink" what the next letter
would be and then the next number.

The more we switch between tasks, the longer we take
to accomplish each task. Multitasking is simply a phony
concept which deludes people into believing they are more
productive when, in fact, they are less productive. In addi-

tion to this self-imposed problem, there is the problem of telephones ringing, walk-ins to the office, and alerts going off (we shall deal with the alerts problem in chapter 8), etc. How then can we avoid this problem?

The answer lies in learning to focus on one item at a time. This reduces the amount of wasted time getting back on track with multiple items. But like trying to break any an addiction, trying to break this habit "cold turkey" can be frustrating.

Perhaps there is a way to change our habits. Perhaps if we can learn to block our time into small concentrated segments, we can learn to focus on one thing at a time and increase our productivity. It just so happens that there is a way to do this.

HELP IN THE FORM OF AN ITALIAN TOMATO

Most people who have spent any time in and around the kitchen, are familiar with the concept of an egg timer. This is typically a simple device originally used to time the cooking of an egg.

In Italy, they refer to this timer by the Italian word for tomato—Pomodoro—referring to timing the cooking of a very basic element in Italian food. The concept is the same as an egg timer. By learning to block our time into focused segments using something as simple as a timer, we can begin to increase productivity one task at a time.

How does this work? First, choose a method for timing your work. Asking Siri (or whatever your phone voice is called) or using a special Pomodoro app found in the app store. There are several of these for each of the different smart phones that use apps. It can be a timer in your phone, tablet or watch. Or it can simply be an old-fashioned timer sitting on your desk.

As you're preparing to do a task, simply set the timer to the desired amount of time you wish to focus on that task. Do not allow yourself to be interrupted from that particular task until the timer goes off (we will take a look at how to deal with interruptions next). When the timer goes off, make a note of what you're thinking or doing so that you can return to it after a short break.

Set the timer for a small break, and move away from where you were working to do something unrelated to that task (for example; get a drink of water, coffee, or head for the restroom).

There really is no universally accepted amount of time for working and breaking. The numbers that most often get suggested, and work well for me, is 25 minutes of work followed by a 5 minute break. This pattern can be repeated up to four times before a longer break is recommended. After four Pomodoro's (roughly 2 hours) a 20-minute break may be an order.

I found an app that allows me to set any amount of work and break time that I choose. At the end of each Pomodoro, the app inserts a 25-minute note in my calendar of what I did for that 25 minutes. Unfortunately, this app is no longer supported within the USA app store. However, there are still a number of Pomodoro apps out there with varying features. If you choose to use one of these apps, I'm sure you can find one that will work for you. I'm beginning to favor the "Hey, Siri. Set a 25-minute timer" approach and then manually record what the time actually produced.

Using this method of breaking work into focused segments will increase productivity.

There have been days when I have gotten as much done in four Pomodoro's as I use to accomplish in an eight-hour day.

I recommend this blocking of your time as it will magnify your focus time. Now what about those distractions?

LEARNING TO SIDE RAIL DISTRACTIONS

The safest and easiest way to deal with distractions is a simple pen and paper sitting beside you as you work.

When a distraction happens, and these can be random thoughts that are off-topic. Simply grab the pen, write an abbreviation of the thought, and return what you're doing.

As a general rule, if you do not allow yourself to be distracted more than a few seconds, you'll have a much better chance of keeping the flow what you were doing before the interruption.

Caveat: answering the phone will defeat the intention of a Pomodoro. The caller will force your brain into a new line of thinking and require *recovery time* to get back to what you were doing, thus slowing you down. Learn to use voicemail and return calls when you can *batch* them together at time more of your convenience. More on batching later.

One of the first things we must learn to do is defeat all alerts coming from our computers, tablets and phones. If you allow alerts to constantly distract you, you will simply be less productive for the same reason multitasking is less productive.

One of the benefits to text messaging and email, as well as all forms of social media, is that they will be waiting for us when we choose to deal with them. Alerts defeat this concept and return us to the problem that plagues pre-voicemail phone calling.

If someone besides you has control over an alert, turn the alert off and deal with it when it fits their schedule rather than theirs (unless your job description demands you be instantly responsive).

OFFICE DISTRACTIONS

A few years ago, a new paradigm in office design became all the rave. It didn't take long to realize that the wizards behind the concept were more interested in social interaction than productivity. The experiment involved taking down cubicles and putting desks so that they faced each other with no physical barriers. The immediate result was that productivity declined. The only thing that increased we're distractions interruptions.

Interacting with people is an important part of our lives. I don't mean to push the idea of becoming a recluse. What I am suggesting is that socializing and work productivity need to be separated as much as possible. There will be the need to interact with other workers. But controlling these interactions is the key to increase productivity.

SOCIAL SAM AND CHATTY KATHY

What about those colleagues who feel free to start talking to you without invitation? This is a common problem where most of us work.

Learn not to make immediate eye contact with the interrupter. Making immediate eye contact shows a form of approval. You do not want to approve this behavior, or you will simply get more of it. Learn that it is not impolite for you to delay the acknowledgment of the interruption until you finish your current thought. Perhaps you even make a note to yourself to reduce *recovery time*. Now turn slowly to the one trying to talk to you, smile and say, "Now, how may I help you?" This sends the message that you have been interrupted from something you were doing. The reason I suggest smiling is for social reasons. Turning with a scowl sends an entirely different message.

Hopefully, this will reduce interruptions. At a minimum, it will at least discourage this type of interaction in the future

SUMMARY POINTS

- Begin using the Pomodoro Approach

- Prove to yourself the Myth of Multitasking by taking the two sentence challenge

- Start focusing on one thing at a time, and put the rest on a list

- Learn to deal with Social Sam and Chatty Kathy

6

CHARACTERISTICS OF A GOOD ORGANIZATIONAL TOOL

Let's talk about how we pull these concepts together. There are five very important characteristics that must be a part of any personal management plan and organizational tool. These must work effectively together and must be 1) accessible, 2) convenient, 3) have triggers, 4) work within a realistic timeframe, and 5) be a single system.

LET'S START WITH ACCESSIBLE

For years people have used large desk pad calendars, calendars that hang on the wall, marker boards, refrigerator placards, picture calendars from an insurance agent, etc. The basic problem with this type of tool is that it is not *accessible* at all times. This means they are not mobile. If you're not near these items when you have ideas to record, then some temporary holding place must be used until you get back to these immobile tracking systems. Unfortunately, the temporary holding place is usually your memory. As we have already discussed this is the most unreliable form of organization.

Another issue associated with these tracking systems is that when you are away from them, you do not know what is already scheduled. Therefore, you could schedule a conflicting event.

> Unfortunately, many people are using the *S.O.S.* system. This stands for *Stack Of Stuff*, and represents the worst of all ideas. When items are stacked in piles before us (things to remember, accomplish, file or forward) we lose convenience and accessibility. In addition, we spend more time looking at and being distracted by these items when we should be concentrating on another task.

The only organizational tool that will function well for the efficient time manager is one that is "at the ready" at any given moment. *Never trust your memory.* It is the weakest link in any organizational plan. The goal is to have the **least** amount of time between thinking a thought and recording it. This takes stress off the brain.

Now we should consider what types of tools can collect data, thoughts, to-dos, and/or appointments at any given moment. The tool you choose will largely reflect personal preference.

It is somewhat like deciding which car to purchase. Although there are some basic decisions about the function of a vehicle, what you purchase really comes down to personal preferences over things like size, mileage, color, interior, trim, sound system, and other options. The same is true for an organizational tool.

Let's consider some of the options currently available. There are paper calendars in a variety of sizes, smart phones, tablets of various sizes and some smaller, lightweight laptops.

Apple admits that the slowing of sales on their iPad Mini is directly attributable to the increase in the size of their iPhone. As the screen size of the phone approached the screen size of the small tablet, many people decided they didn't need two similar devices. Of course, for years laptops have come with a plethora of screen sizes and weights. Most modern laptops have replaced hard drives with flash memory and have eliminated disc drives making them much lighter in weight. Some are trying a "crossover" approach by having a laptop double as a tablet.

Let me go back to the paper calendar for a moment. Many people still prefer pen/pencil and paper. I get this. Writing something down makes us think longer about it. This is why many golfers prefer to walk the course rather than riding a cart. The time it takes to walk to their ball gives them more time to mentally focus on how the next shot might be played (and more exercise). This is a good reason for preferring to write something down.

What I do want to caution against is writing something down in order to make it easier to remember. Remembering what we have to do and where we have to be is exactly what we're trying to avoid. **Never write something down in order to help you remember it. Write something down in order to deliberately forget it.** This requires having confidence that you know where you captured the information. It can't be random.

In other words, let the load be carried by the tool rather than the brain. The brain is the worst organizing tool ever! I say this multiple times, but it is the most common error I see in personal management of time. I'll say more about this under the section on triggers.

How much paper space will you need if you were going to use a paper system? While pocket calendars contribute to the concept of carry convenience, they tend to lack enough space to record all the data that is coming and going from your brain each day. If you're going to use a paper system, I recommend you skip all of the smaller versions and go directly to an 8.5 x 11, two page-per-day tool. This has two advantages. Number one, it includes enough space to keep track of what happens/should happen in a day. Number two, if a person needs to handle paper documents, they will likely be 8.5 x 11. It is much simpler to punch and insert, or remove and file them from a binder already that size than if you are using a smaller paper size.

One thing to remember when purchasing a paper organizer is that the <u>printed sections should not bind you into a predetermined box that does not work for you</u>. If there is a section that calls for daily expenditures of money, and you are not out on the road making reimbursable or tax deductible, daily expenditures, then write in that section something that is more useful to you such as an inspirational thought du jour. If you are going to use a paper organizer, make it work for *you*.

LET'S MOVE TO CONVENIENCE

The second characteristic for an organizational tool is *convenience*. By this I mean the tool should be easy to use. I only intend to address external characteristics at this point. I will address the internal characteristics under the last point; a single system.

Generally speaking, and this may be changing, laptops are slower at waking up, which makes them less convenient for entering and retrieving data. This makes them less convenient. Until that completely changes, the decision for convenience leans toward tablets and phones (and paper). Smart watches are becoming what phones and tablets have become. I expect them to be completely independent devices that do not rely on phones or other computing devices in the not-too-distant future. If you can access your organizational information quickly and easily with an electronic device, then that device would qualify as convenient. If you're technologically challenged, you may be one of the pen and paper people. No shame in that. I like to remind folks it's not about the tool. It's about productivity.

Choose something that fits your lifestyle. Just make sure it's convenient.

NEXT LET'S DISCUSS TRIGGERS

I keep beating the drum of moving away from remembering. I can't think of a single point of TM that causes more stress and more missed appointments, opportunities and to-dos than trying to remember. The second worst is recording items and then failing to check or forgetting where it is recorded.

Enter *triggers*. Just like any firearm, a trigger makes something else happen. If you are into chemistry, think of a catalyst. The easiest way I know to take the stress away from remembering is to have your appointments and tasks remind you at the appropriate time. Those using a paper based system give up this one feature and replace it with a routine of checking. Those using electronic devices still need a routine of checking for that which has not yet been scheduled.

These triggers must be limited to items important to you and must not be allowed to expand to what isn't important to you, but merely distracts you with "alerts" triggered by others. One of the first things to do on any of your devices is eliminate all alerts triggered by someone other than you (or someone for whom your job description requires you to be instantly responsive). This includes social media, email, text messages and anything else that is not what your priorities and plans dictate. You need to be in complete control of your triggers.

> Email is one area that frustrates many people due to email flags. Email flags indicate an importance or intention to deal with something at a later time, but lack the trigger to indicate when that action is to be taken.

How many flagged emails do you currently have in your email? I would bet that many of them have been there far too long. This is a great example of a good idea that lacks a trigger. Instead of flagging an email, replace flagging with a method that prompts action. A trigger does exactly that. If you know when you're going to do something, drag (or copy and paste) that item into your appointment calendar at the appropriate time, setting both a beginning and an ending time for how long it will take. If you do not know exactly when you intend to take the action, then drag (or copy and paste) that item into your to-do list under the appropriate sub-list awaiting scheduling.

Any to-do list worth its salt will allow you to set triggers at the time you wish to be reminded. Look for that app or program that will allow you to set daily, weekday, weekend and any customizable reminders. In my world, it is equally important that I be able to set the time zone, and whether the item should float with the time zone or stay static regardless of time zone. For example, my morning routine reminders need to be at the same time each day regardless of what time zone I'm in. However, phone appointments and meetings usually need to stay static with time zone changes.

In case I wasn't clear before, we are never relieved of the responsibility to check in regularly on our system. But some things do interrupt us because they are time sensitive.

Just make sure the interruption is something you control and determine helpful. Do not let yourself be interrupted by items triggered by social media and friends who have no idea what you are trying to accomplish at the moment. I hear all those "B" personalities who say, "This is what I hate about schedules. They put things ahead of people." Let me say that people are important, but those same people might be appalled that they kept you from something important to you and would gladly have waited if they had just known.

HOW ABOUT A REALISTIC TIMEFRAME?

Many people make unrealistic lists of what they need/want to do without regard to how much time is required. I have been guilty of this. Simply listing to-dos without a *realistic timeframe* is both frustrating and unworkable.

Every time you list something to do, you should estimate a realistic amount of time it will take to do it. This will prevent you from trying to get 18 hours of work done in 10 or 12 hours. My experience says that this leads to a feeling of failure for not getting enough done. It also has a tendency to let unaccomplished tasks bleed over to the next day, compounding the problem. After all, it is time that is finite. Your task list—not so much. When all is said and done, tasks should really be appointments with yourself. They remain on a task list until you have decided when to do them. As soon as you decide when to do them, they should become start/stop calendar appointments that show you how much of your time is already committed. When time runs out, nothing else gets done anyway. Having leftover "to-do's" doesn't help.

FINALLY, YOUR ORGANIZATIONAL TOOL MUST BE A SINGLE SYSTEM

This means that all TM information should be kept in one place. This makes locating as well as retrieving the information **predictable**. Without predictability, we feel like a boat that has had its moorings loosed. We're adrift in open water with too much uncertainty of where we should go or what we should do next.

One of the classic mistakes many people make is trying to keep organizational information in multiple locations. They use multiple apps. They also use scraps of paper. They put some things here. They put somethings there. The result is that they feel overwhelmed. Sound familiar?

How can scientists predict the orbit of the planets? The answer is because the planets are a part of a single solar system. This makes their orbital path predictable. If the planets were not a part of a solar system, their movement through space would become random and unpredictable. This is much like the way many people try to track their organizational information.

In fact, what happens when people keep multiple calendars and to-do lists in various places, is that they push the pressure back on their brain/memory in order to sync all of these together. For example, if someone tries to keep a separate work calendar from their home calendar, they force themselves to remember what is on the other calendar so that they do not create a conflict. Worse, they have to reschedule appointments because they created a conflict.

> When it comes to syncing data located in multiple sources, the area between your ears is not a cloud. It is more like a fog.

It is important at this point to say one more time that the goal is to move our organizational information from our brain/memory onto the organizational tool, not the other way around. David Allen, in his excellent book *Getting Things Done*, simply calls this a collection point. We are less efficient if we have multiple collection points. Often, we're frustrated and stressed.

If you are a paper person, then use only one binder that you have with you at all times. If you are one of the growing list of people using apps (phone, tablet or laptop), then do not have multiple apps all designed to do the similar jobs.

At the moment of this writing, Microsoft is leading the development of an app that does it all. During the heated Apple versus Microsoft wars of previous decades, the two companies went down very divergent points. Microsoft decided to write all-inclusive programs that are huge. Each program Microsoft makes duplicates features from other programs. For example, you can do spreadsheets in Word called *tables*, even though they have a spreadsheet program called Excel. This greatly increases the size and weight of each Microsoft program making them cumbersome.

Apple, on the other hand, decided to go with the "one trick pony" approach. What this means is that no one app on an Apple device is going to do everything needed, at least not yet. The way a person using iOS organizes is by using apps that sync with other apps, sharing information back and forth. By having the information flow between apps, the user still gets the *single system* experience, albeit with some difficulty in getting them to talk to each other in the desired way.

For example, someone might use Apple Mail for their email program, Calendar for their calendar, a to-do list manager for their to-dos and Notes for their stored data. This will only function well if two things are present. One, anything entered on one device automatically syncs with all other devices so that there is no disparity between multiple devices. Google, Microsoft and Apple do a pretty good job here. Two, anything entered in a to-do and given a time to begin and end shows up on the calendar as unavailable time. Hopefully, the calendar shows what the time is dedicated to accomplishing each task and allows you to manipulate the item if necessary. A workaround for this is by forwarding something from one app to another. The goal is to make the process as seamless and easy as possible. Google is currently developing a system that combines Apple and Microsoft techniques. They have multiple programs, all designed to work together, but not exactly in the same way Apple does it.

I suggest you try at least these three big players and see which one makes the most sense for you. Keep in mind that the device you are using will somewhat influence the software application that works best.

If you really want to do some research, get onto the app store and start checking out different apps from lesser known companies. Do not dedicate yourself to one until you have tried several. I don't think there is one yet on the market that does everything. At some point, you are going to have to decide how to fill in gaps.

Summary

- Do you know the 5 characteristics of a good organizational tool?

- Are you ready to reject the "Stack of Stuff" methodology?

- Are you aware that you are more effective when you write everything down so that you can deliberately forget?

- Does your system have triggers that relieve the stress of remembering?

- Have you rejected email flags that do not include triggers?

THE CONTENT OF A GOOD ORGANIZATIONAL TOOL

What does an organizational tool would actually look like? What are the parts that make up a well-planned organization tool?

I'll address both paper and electronic methods with the understanding that apps are constantly being updated with features added or adjusted. Keep in mind that convenience and simplicity of use are two of the top priorities for an organizational tool.

Contacts

In my opinion, the first step in moving from paper to the digital age is to move your contact file into electrons. *Enter the electronic contact file.*

Moving your contacts to digits is the easy part. The most significant issue you will face is making sure your contact list integrates easily into your organizational tool. Next, choose a digital contact list you can live with. If you don't like the application, odds are you're not going to update it. Some people will use a contact list with email applications, while others will use applications found in the app store or GooglePlay. A good contact tool will keep track of a person's name, nickname, multiple phone numbers separating work phone from home phone from mobile phone, etc., work and home addresses, personal information and a notes section for miscellaneous information.

A good example of a product that accomplishes these goals is Microsoft Outlook. Outlook is not only a desktop application, but is also accessible via smart phones and tablets. Each of these sync with one another and do a good job of *integrating* with other organizational information.

However, Microsoft is not the most user-friendly application, but the power to achieve organization is there if you are willing to commit the time to learn the system. Apple, on the other hand decided to go with single function applications that typically serve one purpose and then integrate with other applications to produce various outputs.

MASTER TO-DO LIST

A master to-do list is tricky to organize. The key is to prioritize the tasks. There are methodologies in which to achieve this. The best one I have found so far, I learned from the late Stephen Covey. His suggestion is to organize to-dos according to *roles*. He suggests that most people cannot handle more than six roles effectively. This suggestion has worked well for me over the years.

For example, you might have a role for work, another for home/personal/family, another might be church/charity/non-profit, another for recreational/sports/hobby, etc.

Each time you want to record a to-do, you would simply put it under the correct role.

In addition to roles, you want a method of being able to capture what has come to be called a **context**. These are individualized according to your life, but might include such things as: Brainstorming/Ideas/Quadrant 2 (Important Not Urgent) thinking, Menial/Low-energy, Routines (daily, weekly, monthly, quarterly, semi-annual, annual, etc.), Phone calls, etc.

Each item in a master to-do list is thus categorized with a *role* and a context in which to accomplish it. The role helps one enter information in an organized way. The *context* becomes a way to group or *batch* things so that they can be accomplished more efficiently.

Batching is always more efficient than bouncing between dissimilar actions. Returning all your phone calls at one time it's far more efficient than returning them one at a time sandwiched between other things. Hence, the term *batching*.

The idea is to record anything you have to do as well as anything you want to do. Assign it a role, context, and estimated time to accomplish. These lists will build, but each week some of them will be moved to your calendar. Items not making this week's list simply wait their turn until their priority dictates they be moved to the calendar and completed.

When disasters strike and destroy your plan, simply move a few items back to the Master Task List as unaccomplished.

Moving between a task list and a calendar is a convenience worth pursuing. Outlook is improving on this function. Apple doesn't have a convenient way to integrate tasks and calendar as of yet. I personally use a 3rd party app such as OmniFocus2 to do this.

Q2 QUADRANT 2 (IMPORTANT NOT URGENT) THINKING/RANDOM IDEAS

Even though a master to do list contains a context for doing things, it is important to have a place to record brainstorming and long-range critical thinking. There is typically a period of time between when an idea occurs and when we decide to take action. Think of it as an incubation list for your thoughts. The idea remains on this list until it is ready for additional thought or execution. Paper usually has the advantage over apps in this situation.

Very few apps have adequate space to record important thoughts that are not ready for action. Having a place to record random thoughts, scheduling time to do Quadrant 2 (Important Not Urgent) thinking, and reviewing these thoughts on a regular schedule is a characteristic of leaders who are forward thinkers.

THE EISENHOWER MATRIX

	URGENT	NOT URGENT
IMPORTANT	**QUADRANT 1** IMPORT AND URGENT	**QUADRANT 2** IMPORTANT BUT NO URGENT
NOT IMPORTANT	**QUADRANT 3** URGENT BUT NOT IMPORTANT	**QUADRANT 4** NOT IMPORTANT AND NOT URGENT

Most apps lack dedicated space for this activity. At best you have use a place intended for something else. I use an iOS-only app called OmniFocus2. Because it has an "Inbox," I am able to use this area for unclassified thoughts not ready for action. It's not perfect, but it serves the purpose. Other alternatives might include: OneNote or Apple Notes

CALENDAR

(planned & actual)

As you know, calendars display dates and times. At the end of the day everything we do requires time. The calendar is not just a place to schedule meetings. It is also a place to quantify a plan by comparing the time we can schedule to accomplish a task and the actual time available to accomplish the task.

In other words, all tasks will eventually be translated to calendar appointments in order to realistically make sure there is adequate time to do them.

Think of tasks as "appointments with your work." The personal discipline of scheduling comes easy for some people, but not for others. Your personality type and routines will have significant influence on the type of scheduler/calendar you use.

If you are a linear type of person, you will lean toward a traditional calendar with its rigid time blocks. If your style is nonlinear, you may decide that mind mapping better represents your time space continuum

At the end of the chapter is an example of the traditional calendar approach as well as an example using the mind mapping methodology. Either way, you may want to consider having a general theme for each day. For example, Monday could be the day you try to schedule meetings. Tasks of a more menial nature could be pushed toward Tuesday. Writing might be on Wednesday, etc. This is meant as a general guide since it is rarely possible to be 100% pure in this approach.

For example:

Monday: Meetings & Menial Tasks
Tuesday: Priority Tasks (larger blocks)
Wednesday: Writing
Thursday: Think Strategically
Friday: Finalize what got interrupted

An ideal calendar would let you record both what was planned and how the plan worked out in reality. I have a separate diary type app for recording what did happen. It is not as convenient as having both side by side within the same app, but I make it work

The biggest mistake I see people make is trying to make plans in multiple locations. Never keep more than one calendar. This is a disaster waiting to happen.

Microsoft allows one calendar to display different colors. Each role can be assigned a separate color. This makes it easier to glance at a calendar and see the different roles occupying your day. For example, if a doctor's appointment is scheduled during work hours, that color will jump out at you because you're not used to seeing a personal color during work time.

If you work in a "shared calendar" environment, make sure you do not make your personal appointments visible to others. They should only be able to see a generic blocked out time when you are not available, without being able to see the details of what the appointment is or even the role assigned.

DIARY OF WHAT ACTUALLY HAPPENED TODAY (WHₐT)

One of the great parts about having an organizational system, is that it provides the opportunity and space to journal our daily activities. It doesn't matter what you call this journal. Call it a daily journal (DJ), a daily record of events (DRE), my day's activities (MDA) or what happened today (WHT).

Journaling your activities, meetings and accomplishments throughout the day is the icing on the cake of personal organization. Even if you never use this information there will be an indirect bump in productivity just knowing you have recorded, and will record, what happens in your day.

Later in the book we will examine a more direct method of linking the daily journal to increased productivity. Voice recognition software is another method to journal your events.

LONG-RANGE GOAL PLANNING

With the exception of low-level strategic Quadrant 2 (Important Not Urgent) thinking, everything we've talked about involves short-range actions. Let me ask you how you think it would work out if you drove a vehicle while only looking a few feet in front of your front bumper as you sped down a highway. Not pretty, right? If we do enough Quadrant 2 (Important Not Urgent) thinking/dreaming, some of those thoughts will develop into goals. The only way to set and stay a course is to have a final destination determined. Short-range decisions and actions need to work toward a longer-range thinking.

Most people will ask themselves questions like "Where do I want to be at the end of my life? What about the end of my career? In 10 years? Five years? This time next year?"

From a personal standpoint, this used to be in the front, not the back, of my paper planner. I wanted to be constantly reminded to keep the long-range goal(s) in mind when establishing the shorter-ranged (weekly) plan. No matter where or how you keep track of these, it is essential they be in front of you and seen frequently for planning purposes.

Many people allow themselves to be sucked into doing the bidding of a job or the requests of colleagues and family without having an overall strategy that prevents life regret in later years. Life just becomes a series of random acts following what is in front of our face and what others decide.

Now that I have organized and planned electronically, I use a weekly reminder to review and edit my goals. This reminder comes just before my weekly planning so that I'm conscious of the desired long-term end. I do not want to go more than a week without seeing these goals so that I have a better chance of staying on course, so to speak.

Longer range goals do not change much. They tend to only need infrequent course corrections. However, if I do not review them regularly, I find myself drifting away from actions that take me toward them. If I review them just before planning my week, I stay true (or closer) to the course I desire. Sure, work often demands menial or "others-oriented" tasks. But without that constant review, fewer items on my weekly plan would keep me headed toward my goals. In chapter 8 we will take a closer look at how to set long-range goals and work toward making part of our weekly plan.

DOCUMENT STORAGE

Ideally, an organizational tool also keeps track of documents generated during a day. Most of the personal management apps that I have tried are deficient in this as well. The work-around solution is to use a storage place that can easily store and retrieve documents, photos, etc. in a remote location, but be readily accessible. Perhaps consider Evernote, Dropbox, GoogleDrive, iCloud, or OneDrive as a work around. Use the one that requires the least amount of clicking or typing. The goal is to relieve as much manual input and automate the process as much as possible.

Evernote has a feature where a special email address can send any file into a generic, "catch-all" folder. This is a great feature, but does require further sorting at a time when one actually opens the Evernote app. This must be done manually in Evernote, but at least it can be done. Most of these storage apps have a monthly or annual fee based on capacity.

Some apps allow you to attach files. Others allow a hyperlink to access documents. Play around with a few before choosing one. Remember, riding two horses at one time is tricky at best, and dangerous at worst. It can be very frustrating wasting time sitting because you are delayed at the airport or another location without access to documents.

If you get stuck in a time robbing situation, use it to your advantage by retrieving and working on documents. This eliminates wasted time.

The scenario above is also a chance to review unscheduled items and/or provide them context. Many of the more menial tasks in a day can actually be accomplished with available "in between" time in a day you couldn't foresee. These must be listed and put on a calendar, but often get done at a time different than you planned.

Remember that accessibility along with convenience is what makes the time management system work

If at any time you can access your organizer to make adjustments, you are working from something that will both relieve your stress and keep you feeling more in control of your time. All of this pre-supposes that your organizer is accessible and convenient at virtually all times.

Although quite extreme, I have a friend that uses a waterproof organizer and even takes it in the shower. Why? Because sometimes our best thoughts come at unexpected or inconvenient times. I certainly applaud the concept of not trying to hang on to a thought while our brain is still in high gear going from thought to thought. How often do we forget a good thought because we allowed ourselves to drift into other thoughts?

That doesn't mean I'm ready to schedule from the shower. With voice activated reminders, I could capture that brilliant thought or solution to a problem from the shower just by calling out to my phone.

Time is fixed. Manage yourself.

Here is an example of a tradition calendar. It is linear in concept and gives a good visual of any view (weekly is shown). If your work has many self-appointments within an hour's time, perhaps working from the daily view with 15-minute divisions would work better. Just remember, most people use a calendar only for appointments with other people. A calendar should really represent the plan you have for yourself. Most of your appointments are going to be with yourself.

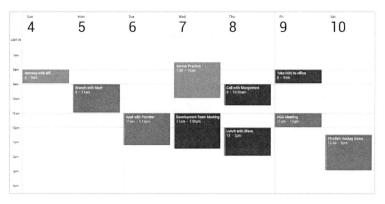

Some folks don't function well in a linear structure. I get that. So how could someone who favors a more non-linear approach still get organized? Enter the mindmap.

A mindmap allows for a free flow approach to organization. This example below is a radial (clockwise) setup. Some prefer a top-down mindmap where each day or role has single action items below them in

Notice that there are really two mindmaps here. The first is organizing action items under the concept of roles. The second is a general approach to which part of which day the action is intended (even those who favor the linear approach need a way to identify actions by roles).

This approach is for those who recoil at setting specific times and following a traditional calendar. In this approach, I would use the mindmap to drag action items back and forth between what I planned to do and when I planned to do it. If someone needs help, I have the flexibility to drag an item to another general time or back onto the action list until I can plan a time.

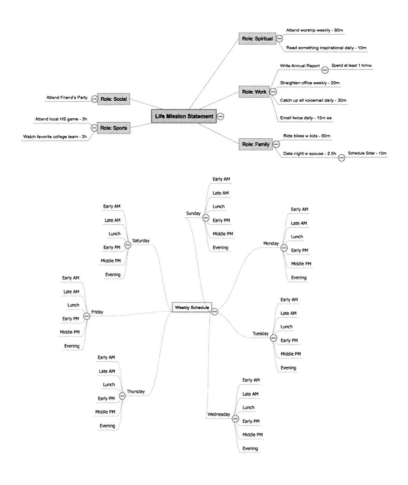

SUMMARY

- Do you operate with a complete, but single system for collecting all your important appointments and tasks?

- Have you decided to reject the S.O.S. method of working from a "Stack of Stuff?

- Have you learned how to mindmap your ideas?

- Have you learned how to turn those ideas into a workable schedule ?

8

SOCIAL MEDIA/EMAIL

Today's world is filled with social media. Some of it is productivity-friendly. Some of it is a complete side rail from the main track of productivity—i.e. bad personal management. Everyone needs to evaluate social media for what it does for them, not what it does for the company that is promoting the social media program.

Here's an idea. Think of social media as a pet alligator. You might enjoy feeding your pet alligator or taking it for a walk, but you had better also keep in mind that it is an alligator and should be respected as one or it will eat you for lunch.

Years ago, before social media, there was "the news." News was on at a specific time. You could tune in to radio or television and catch a broadcast concerning what the commentators thought was important. Then it expanded. Really expanded. Local news got its own slot. National news got another slot. World news got yet another.

Today we are in what has been described as a 24/7/365 news cycle. No one can watch news constantly. Nor should they. Knowing what is going on is a good thing. Being consumed by what is going on is a bad thing.

Enter sports. No longer is there a "big game of the week." Rather, there are too many to track. Some try to keep track of multiple sports. Some follow professional and college sports. There seems to be 24/7/365 in sports just like news. Those who do keep up have a large chunk of time dedicated to that task. Very few are earning money or advancing a career by doing so.

Now apps "alert" you anytime something happens that could be called news, sports, Hollywood development (scandal), or even when your friends are doing something. All of this incoming information has to be managed effectively.

You have probably already found that social media has replaced much of what used to be handled as email. Email began as what is now called a tweet. It was short and could not handle attachments. People began clamoring for longer character limits. Then the pressure came for document attachments. Soon the demand resulted in the capability to send photos and videos. Email became huge. Email became a business tool. Email became overwhelming. Email began to eat up too much of the day as important messages got mixed in with not so important messages. Messages could get marked "urgent" even when they weren't. Folks didn't follow the protocol of the To recipient for intended action, and the CC recipient for information only. Like the early concept of a paperless society, email began to be overused and misused until it became a pet alligator. Enter the Tweet. Tweeting is what email was originally intended to be, a short message.

Still, it is helpful to think of email in the vein of social media, albeit an early version. Email is necessary for most businesses as it allows near instantaneous delivery of messages, documents, photos, etc.

The beginning point is to evaluate how much time you're spending on email. Do you have control or is it out of control?

There is an old Hindu proverb that says, "He who rides on the back of a tiger must never get off." For some, email has become that tiger.

The next action is to evaluate social media for what it can do *for* you instead of what it does *to* you. Although this may mean unfollowing and unfriending some social media connections, there is another way that won't seem so radical. Schedule your viewing of non-productive social media away from times you need to be getting something done. Since it is very easy to get distracted by what isn't important (all mixed in with what is important), one idea might be to schedule a social media appointment once or twice a day. However, you must balance your work and social media interaction. Failure to do so can have significant consequences. Set an appointment with a beginning time and an ending time. Have your phone go off when your time is up and make yourself break away. You must break the social media addiction. Remove the curiosity and rush to have someone like or respond to your post.

Let's start with Facebook. More and more folks are finding a way to sell and build a contact database using Facebook. Early on, companies were encouraging customers to "like us on Facebook" as a way to drive folks to a website and/or market to them.

The problem with Facebook is that business and social aspects are interwoven with one another. If you do not learn how to use Facebook for business and you give into the social aspects, chances are Facebook makes you unproductive.

Some people are capable of ignoring personal messages during business hours while other cannot resist the temptation. Those that cannot resist the temptation might want to consider setting up two separate Facebook accounts. One professional and one personal. This will help keep the information separate and distinct.

If you are tech-savvy enough, or can get someone who is, you can forward professional messages to some other business oriented location, such as a website. In that case, one account might work for you. You are not actually viewing social media, but are only viewing the collection point of what you want out of social media.

Let's take a look at Twitter. It is an endless supply of time-consuming tweets.

Like watching a river, Twitter is non-stop. But what does reading all those tweets actually do for you? If you are selective, it can keep you abreast of developments in your industry or trends that will affect your life. Or the opposite can be true.

Twitter is probably the hardest to use productively until you learn how to forward the tweets that matter without having to scroll through the ones that don't.

Except in the rarest of circumstances, I would reject Twitter as a way to do business. Exceptions would be media personnel, those who make a living in politics, etc. Otherwise consider Twitter something for your personal life and avoid it while you are working.

The same goes for Snapchat, Instagram, and similar social media apps and sites. These are wonderful ways to keep up with family (one of the largest growing demographics in social media are parents and grandparents who have discovered they can track their offspring on social media) and friends, but are dubious when it comes to making them work for business.

Again, if you are using these social media programs to build a database of customers, it might be considered a justifiable use. Let's be honest though. It is not easy to use the programs listed in the previous paragraph for attracting those who do not know you on a personal basis. Only you can decide. But please be honest with yourself when making these decisions.

Before I leave the subject of social media entirely, let me address television. With cable, dish, etc. it is possible to have hundreds of channels.

Are you a movie junkie? Multiple channels go from one movie to another, as do sports and news. Ad infinitum. Whatever your appetite, it is available constantly. How will you tame this potential beast?

One idea is to schedule once a week what you want to watch for the coming week. Record it and watch it when it fits your schedule. This keeps you from watching something you don't really care about while neglecting something you should care about.

Do you sit and watch commercials? If you record a program, you can usually get past the commercials. I once watched a recorded football game in 52 minutes. The playing time is 60 minutes. The network schedule was 180 minutes. By fast-forwarding from tackle to huddle break, I actually got through the game and the commercials in less than the actual playing time. I might have gotten through it even faster, except I did back up and re-watch two spectacular plays.

That might be anathema to some, thinking they want to spend 3 hours relaxing. Well, if that is your intended goal, then efficiency is not. I leave that to you. I'm guessing that announcers probably don't want to hear that I didn't need their explanation of what I just saw, but I was pleased.

SUMMARY

Action items:

- Right now, lay the book down and pick up your phone. Go to the settings and find each social media app. Check the alert settings for each and make sure they are contributing to your productivity and not distracting you from it.

- Monitor your use of social media for a week and see how much time you're actually viewing it. You may be shocked.

- Schedule times to check social media when it is right for you. A couple of times a day should be sufficient for personal use.

- Consider if having two accounts for some social media apps would help keep you from wasting productive time on personal information. Do you know how to do that? Do you know someone who does? Would the money you save from time no longer wasted justify paying someone to set this up for you?

- Rethink your use of TV. Make it serve you and not the other way around.

Don't just let the thought go. Do something about it. Now.

DELEGATION

The ability to delegate or duplicate yourself in others can really make efficient use of your time. People make several excuses for failing to delegate. The most common excuses tend to be: (1) I don't trust others to do a good job (2) Everyone is busy or just as busy as I am (3) I don't want others to think I am laying my work off on them (4) I can do it myself in less time than it takes to explain and monitor someone else, etc.

Let's start with thinking you can do something in the same amount of time it would take to show someone else and train them.

This is usually a problem of myopia—a short-sighted view of the long game.

The more you work with someone else to get something done, the more they get to understand your standards and expectations.

Eventually, you will recapture the time because there are more hands that can do the work. The longer you continue to do a job that should not be exclusively yours, the longer it will be before someone else will have to learn to do it.

That begs the question: what would happen if you were indisposed? What if this job needs to be done when you are sick or on vacation? God forbid, what if you die? Or change jobs? Who is going to do it then? Why not start with them now before the crisis? In other words, you aren't just thinking about this time, but all the times that will come later. It may not be this exact job, but there will be others like it. Start spending your time making it possible to duplicate your effort in others.

Secondly, let's address not trusting others. Many of those who have a problem with delegating do so because they compare where they are now, later in their learning curve, with where the other person is now, at the beginning of their learning curve.

Think back to when you were first learning to do a particular task. Chances are you hesitated, took extra time to think about something, made bad choices, etc.

Now, after a learning curve, you can do that job fast and efficiently. Bravo.

Now give your trainee the same consideration. Give them time to figure things out. Allow them to hesitate, be unsure before they are confident. By doing so, you are on your way to getting them to where you are now. Additionally, instead of focusing on what you believe to be the lack of skill, experience or motivation in others, why not focus on your own ability to communicate clearly and motivate others?

This allows you to focus on what you can control, instead of wasting your time on what you can't control (internals in others).

Allow me to pause and insert something here. There are tasks that should not be delegated. For example, if you have to deliver some bad news, a reprimand, a bad performance review, or even a termination of a direct report, that should probably not be delegated. <u>Be careful handing over jobs that should belong to you. But quit holding onto those jobs that should not belong to you.</u> Because you are not going to delegate jobs that should not be delegated, you will begin to see that the lower down a task can be handled, the more efficient the process.

What about the excuse that you don't want to be seen as laying off work on others that you don't want to do? Very simply make sure you keep an appropriate number of tasks, many unpleasant, that you choose not to delegate this time around in order to balance the workload. Next time, you delegate what you did this time. You won't be seen as lazy if others realize sometimes you do it, but other times you delegate it.

That means you must learn how to communicate clearly and effectively for the outcome you desire. Rarely will you want to dictate the method for getting something done. Perhaps this might be necessary in the beginning of phase 1 (see diagram). Mostly you want to delegate outcome and let the person to whom you delegated work out their own process.

Look at the diagram below. It basically demonstrates the 4-phase process required to delegate effectively.

I do not think you should expect to get to phase 4 with every direct report. There is a trust level, and definitely a time factor, involved in moving through each phase.

Experience tells me that the biggest hang-ups to effective delegation happen at phases one and four. By this I simply mean that too many people reject phase one because it requires the time of two people to do what one person could do if this were the only desired outcome. However, you are learning that this is not the only desired outcome. You have this task and the training of the other person for future tasks as your parallel goals. You should gladly sacrifice twice the man-hours on this task because of how many of your hours can be saved in the future.

The other hang-up occurs when someone tries to skip phases one, two and three and simply expect another person to be able to follow your instructions and expectations without the requisite time to get through the other phases.

Know that these phases are sequentially ordered for the purpose of learning and building trust. Therefore, you cannot skip a phase. Each phase allows you and the other person to get comfortable with one another as well as the task being trained. Gaining insight into what is unique to you and your expectations is something the other person is struggling to learn.

Let's look at two examples:

- you have 50 copies of a 10-page document that have to be collated by hand.

Let's say you communicate (in your mind it is clear what you intend) that there are no page numbers on the documents, but there is a specific order you wish to have them.

Perhaps you make the first set yourself while the other person watches. You put that one out as a guide in case they get confused. You suggest they keep it separate so that it may be used as a reference.

Now let's suppose the other person chooses to start with the last page and put each page on top of the one to follow. This is backwards to how you did the sample, but the outcome is the same. No problem. If that works better for them, the process is not important. The outcome is important.

- Now let's suppose the task is setting up equipment that needs security cables to lock them down to prevent theft.

It is important to you that the security cables be placed and locked at the very beginning of the process so that there is minimal time between valuable equipment being exposed and it being secured. Having shown the other person how and why you want the security cables installed first, you ask them to do it the next time while you watch. They set up several pieces of equipment before getting around to the security cables. Now you remind them that the order of the process is important for this task. Security cables need to be done, not later. This is to prevent getting distracted and leaving expensive equipment vulnerable to theft. Now the process is important to you and they need to know it is important to you. Perhaps you say, "Once the expensive equipment is secured by the cables, I do not care what order you use." You are communicating that some of the process is important to you.

SUMMARY

- Think through a typical workday. What tasks are repetitive and could be done by others so that you can do what others cannot do?

- Try delegating one to three items from your regular workday. You may find others can do some things better than you.

- Expect an initial hit on your time as you communicate your expectations and the final outcome desired. Don't let that stop you from the long-game of making yourself more effective.

MAKING SPACE WORK FOR YOU

Most attempts at personal management do not address a very real problem and one that often costs us a lot of time—messiness.

There is a high price to pay for clutter. Typically, it is not usually obvious at first. We lose time looking for things and it also destroys our mental freedom by creating a distraction.

The more we have in front of us, the more distractions we experience. One of the main reasons we put things in front of us is to remind ourselves to do something later. Once we learn to trust the alerts in our organizer tool the less we will need to create a visual reminder called a *Stack of Stuff*. (See Chapter 6) With an acronym like S.O.S., we can begin to see clutter as a distress call.

Putting things away is a discipline. It requires seeing a clean and organized work space as a valuable part of your work, not a distraction from your work. As long as you see productivity as something other than a clean and organized workspace, you'll struggle with a messy office.

When you begin to see a clean workspace as productive, the struggle to *get more done* will no longer avoid straightening, organizing and cleaning.

Because most people do not see cleanup as productive, most do not take time to put things away. Instead, they pile them in the most convenient place available. Unfortunately, that is usually the most valuable workspace—meaning it is also the most inconvenient place when it comes to accomplishing work. When we use up our workspace for stacking stuff for later, aside from the problem of distracting ourselves, we leave ourselves feeling too cluttered to work effectively and, therefore, have not contributed to our productivity. We have to start seeing organization of our space and putting everything in its place as a means to being more productive.

As a general rule, we humans will fill all available space with something, anything, until there is no space left. The bigger the storage area, the more we store. Papers that should be thrown away are put in open space just because there is space. So here is the rule for anything over which you have control— one-in-one-out. What this means is that every time you bring something into your space, something of equal size has to go out of your space, one-in-one-out. The only alternative is to see the clutter and mess just keep building.

Now I recognize that the pressure of business often makes us put something down to free our hands to do something else.

I also realize that coworkers are often bringing you stuff while you're working on something else. Resist the urge to let piles become your default filing or storage solution.

If that is a problem you have, then beat that habit by scheduling a time to file, organize and cleanup—at least by end of each workday. Set a goal to never leave work without an office, work area, etc. ready for inspection or a visit from the local school.

If you cannot be proud of your work area, you aren't working at your best, most productive level.

LET'S START WITH THE STANDARD OFFICE

Let's imagine a typical office and allow for adjustments to what you actually have in your life. If your situation is slightly different from what I describe, hopefully you can make the application of the idea work in what you actually experience.

Take a moment to assess your office work area. Look at it as if you're seeing it for the first time. Why are items placed where they are? Acknowledge that window, ventilation, electrical outlets can force some arrangements. Not much can be done with these and other "immovable" objects. Large pieces of furniture are sometimes forced into a space that is less desirable from a productivity point of view. We live with these situations even if they aren't the most effective from a productivity standpoint.

But what places other items where they are? A previous oc-cupant had it there? Movers put it there? What I'm asking you to do is think in terms of productivity for the next few minutes.

Somewhere along the way, I ran across what was called the ABC method of arranging a space. It has worked well in offices I have had. I'll describe it in the following way.

Anything you access on a daily basis should be in the most convenient place with no steps required to reach them. This almost always includes a desk, possibly a credenza or table behind us. If we sit at the desk, then what we can reach without getting up is the **A area**. Sit in your desk chair and extend your arms to their fullest. Rotate left and right. That circle is the **A area**. The **B area** is what can be reached with one step. This is the place for items that need to be accessed on a weekly basis. Anything that is used, touched or looked at less than once a week belongs in the **C area**. Simply put, the **C area** is anything beyond **B**." I have additionally added that something stored outside the office is a **D area**. This could be a print room, a shared filing area, a company library/research area, etc.

Having this imaginary circle area around you allows you to rethink why things are where they are.

Let's examine the top of your desk. This is your best work space (perhaps unless you have a work table or L-shaped extension with it). What is occupying this space? Let me guess a com-puter/monitor (I hope not a printer. Unless you print frequently, don't give up your best space to a printer.), a telephone, a light of some kind, a stapler, and in-box (or a stack of baskets for multiple flows), perhaps a "doo-dad" holder of some kind, picture(s), etc. How am I doing so far?

Now ask yourself how often you use the stapler. Should it get your best space? Could the telephone be behind you, on the side of your desk or on a wall? Could the computer/monitor be on a credenza or table behind or beside the desk? Is there a better place for the in-box? Is the lighting in the office so poor a desk lamp is required? How often do you actually turn it on? Could the family pictures be on the wall or a bookshelf?

I'm not telling you what to have on your desk, I'm asking you to evaluate if you are using the space in the best possible way.

My most productive work comes when I'm not fighting the distraction of clutter on my desk. Perhaps you'll experience the same thing if you give it some thought. There is something peaceful and motivating about having a clean workspace.

Is the office large enough to allow a separate work area for the kind of work not particularly suited for sitting at a desk? Would a printer, paper cutter, stapler, hole punch, paper clips, etc. go better in another area (if space allows)?

Next let's take an obvious one—the lap drawer. Most desks have a drawer just above where the chair (and human legs) go. This drawer typically has small compartments for pencils, paper clips, push-pins, and rubber bands.

Now ask yourself if you use pencils, paper clips, push-pins and rubber bands. How often? Most people rarely use these items any more. Yet is it getting some of your best space? Why? The answer is probably because the furniture manufacturer has been building desks that way for years and you felt obligated to go along with a centuries old design. This is your **A area**. Use it wisely.

What else is in that drawer? Chances are it will be items that are rarely used. It's just the handiest storage for items you didn't know where else to put. They don't have a "place." Right now would be a good time to take anything out of the lap drawer that you rarely use and open up the space. Even if you don't know what you will put there, make the space available for later.

Now let's rethink the drawers to the side of the chair. Again, these are in your **A area**. What do you find in them? You may find that you had forgotten what was in them because you so rarely access these items. Begin removing what isn't required on a daily basis. Free this space up for daily items

What about the **B circle**? Take a moment to actually look at what is within a step of your chair. Do you really use this at least weekly?

I see offices with a bookshelf behind the desk, but what is on the bookshelf are items that merely have to be dusted. Having an office that is pleasing to you requires some decorating, but should it be in your **B circle**?

These are productivity choices you have to make for yourself based on your work situation.

You need places to store things that are rarely accessed. Many of the items that came out of your **A** and **B** areas will wind up in the **C area**. Perhaps it is a filing cabinet, a covered bookshelves or actual cabinetry. Everyone has those "don't need them often, but have to keep them" items.

Is your printer a **B area** or a **C area**? I've worked in places where network printers were shared by several people and weren't even in my office. This is why I have invented another area called the **D area** for those items outside the office.

HANDLING MAIL AND OTHER PIECES OF PAPER

Speaking of filing cabinets, let's talk about the bane of office work—filing. How easy is it for you to pile rather than file? Do you believe you're too busy to put things "all the way away?" I used to find this to be a trap. I would have something in my hand, but needed to look something up on the computer. Rather that filing it right then, I would tell myself I'll just lay it on top of the filing cabinet until I complete this lookup. Guess where it stayed far too long? I hate filing. Yet when I do file, I feel so much better about myself and the office.

A number of years ago I read about a study that monitored executives in their normal daily routine. It found that the average executive touched a piece of paper 16 times due to time pressure, indecision and procrastination. This is ridiculous, but commonplace.

We need to be prepared to deal with paper the first time we touch it. Let me offer some suggestions.

First, set yourself a goal to only touch a piece of paper once (allow yourself a second touch if rule number two comes into play). Be prepared the first time you touch a piece of paper to do one of three things:

1. Identify it as low value and trash it immediately.

2. Glean whatever is important from it in less than two minutes and then trash it or file it appropriately. Beware of setting the paper down to "file later."

3. Schedule it now or do it now. Identify it as a more than a two-minute item, schedule exactly when you will deal with it in your place for appointments and to-dos. Include a note there reminding you of where it will be located at the time scheduled. Now place it in the specifically marked area for easy retrieval at the time you scheduled.

Second, make sure you actually have time to deal with your mail before you open it. Most likely learned from GTD to guide me in this matter. If I can read something or deal with it in less than two minutes, I do it immediately. If it is going to take longer than two minutes, then I schedule time to read or deal with it. But the scheduling must happen now, not later. Allow yourself a second touch of the paper on items requiring more than two minutes.[1]

---

1. This rule does not apply to time used for organizing. Stopping organization to accomplish 2 minute tasks defeats the efficiency of organizing.

Third, have your scheduler MAP (my action plan) at the ready. When mail or any other document is going to take longer than two minutes to handle, it needs to either be scheduled or placed in your MAP.

Fourth, use what I call the hesitation rule. If you catch yourself hesitating as to whether something is a valuable for keeping or reading, err on the side of the trashcan. Those things that actually have value are immediately recognizable as valuable. Things that "might" have value probably do not.

Fifth, is location for opening mail. I suggest never opening your mail except over a trash can, because that's where most of it is going. If you do find a piece of mail that needs to be read or dealt with, be prepared to read or deal with it NOW. Putting aside to read later is only good if you actually schedule when you' re going to read it. Otherwise, you' re setting yourself up for the repeated touch of that piece of paper trying to remember what it was and what you should do with it. Just make the decision the first time.

The key is the right mental attitude before you start to deal with mail. Have a "get this box checked off" mentality before you begin.

Paper handling rules:

- ✓ Rule one: the one-touch rule.

- ✓ Rule two: the two-minute rule.

- ✓ Rule three: the hesitation rule.

✓   Rule 4: Hesitation probably means questionable value.

✓   Rule 5: Only open mail near trash can.

One antidote to prevent many touches and messiness is to schedule a filing appointment with yourself. This must almost always be a low-energy time in your circadian rhythm (see Chapter 3).

I will tell you that it must be at least done daily or the dragon will grow too large to slay.

Some folks like a last thing of the day appointment. I like the logic of that idea, although I find it hard for me to practice. Other folks like an "as I return from lunch" appointment. This works better for me because I can get it done before my brain reconnects with the desk and computer. Both times are even better if you have to handle a lot of files and makes the work less burdening.

Now I have described an office with a desk and a chair. Perhaps your work area is different. Perhaps you stand or sit at a workbench, assembly line, or something else. The same principles apply.

Before we leave the office/work area, I would like to suggest five simple ideas to help with the office space management.

Compartmentalize Space

Think in terms of the type of work being done and see if making separate areas for each would increase productivity. Even having a computer/monitor behind you so that you must turn your chair to work at it might increase non-computer work on your desk.

A Place for Everything

We've all heard the admonition *A place for everything, and everything in its place.* Well, that's because it is good advice. When you have items that have no home, they become distractions and often wind up getting moved from place to place—often frequently.

Many of the piles found in offices are simply a result of trying to hang onto something for which there is no home. Tell yourself, "If I'm going to keep it, it needs a permanent home, not a temporary one."

How much stuff in your office is still sitting in the temporary place you put it?

Manage the Incoming

The pressure of business often means much is coming at us. I don't know about you, but email alone can feel like spooning water up a river. Add people bringing you documents, notes from meetings and phone calls and it can become overwhelming.

This is one of those places where not allowing stacks and piles to develop actually becomes a productivity helper. Enter the action in your organizer rather than using the stack to guide your work. Unless you are going to deal with that paper now, get it put away. One idea is to always have an appointment with yourself in your office after each meeting (or series of back-to-back meetings) where you file minutes. Longer time will be scheduled if you have to input the paper notes digitally or rewrite the scribbles. In other words, you don't schedule one hour for a weekly board meeting. You schedule one hour followed by a 15-minute filing. Now you have given yourself a plan to keep better organized.

Ruthlessly Eliminate

I still remember how computers were supposed to give us a paperless society. What a joke. People started printing extra copies of documents. I wound up having both a hard copy and computer copy of the same item. Learn to keep only one if you need to, none if you don't. You will drown in paper if you don't learn to ruthlessly eliminate the unnecessary. I sometimes go into offices and see documents with cobwebs stacked in the corner of the floor or old newspapers because there is "something in there I want to keep for reference." How likely would that person remember what is in the newspaper, let alone where to look later?

Schedule Org/Cleanup Routine

Mentioned earlier in this chapter is having a daily filing/putting away time. I would follow that up with a weekly one as well.

Think about your impression of someone who has a very stacked, piled, cluttered work space. They get things done, but with less efficiency and more mental distractions.

Now think of someone with a very neat, tidy, clean office (surely you know someone who fits this description). What is your impression of them? Chances are you don't suspect that they do nothing. Chances are you secretly envy them.

Set a goal to become the one everyone else envies because your office is the way they wish theirs was.

DO I DARE TALK ABOUT YOUR VEHICLE?

There are three main spaces in the typical vehicle. There is a front-seat area. Most have a back-seat area. Typically, there is a trunk or storage area (or pickup bed).

What could these possibly have to do with personal (time) management? Turns out—quite a bit.

Do you have a clean area visible to you when you drive, or do you have stuff crammed above the visor, crowding the dash and all over the floorboard? Perhaps you've heard the joke about the county workers who wrecked their work truck and sustained no injuries because of all the Styrofoam cups they had on the dash served to cushion their impact. Yeah, that is funny, but a complete distraction.

What is in your glove box? Few people keep driving gloves in there anymore, yet we still call it a glove box. Most folks find very outdated papers, flashlights with dead batteries, and more. Ask yourself how much time it would take to clean this area of your vehicle if you did it regularly. Why not tie your semi-annual routine of updating vehicle proof of insurance with cleaning and organizing your glove box?

Now let's use the ABC method that we talked about in our office. Are there items near your drivers' seat that you rarely use? Then why are they there? You know what to do. The result will likely be a clearer head when you're driving. You might even have inspiration. Just be sure to pull over to record it.

The same goes for the back seat. I see vehicles with the back seat loaded with the same items for months with no change. It sometimes makes me wonder if their fuel mileage would change just by clearing some things out of the back seat.

And what about that trunk/storage area? Have you even looked in there lately?

I think some emergency items make sense. That's essentially what the spare tire is. When was the last time you checked the air pressure in it (sounds like an action item for the quarterly routine list)? Flares or reflectors make sense, as does bottled water rotated at regular intervals. Perhaps some warm clothing or a wool blanket, which can help in cases of shock or cold/damp conditions. Tie some plastic around any of these items to keep them cleaner, then check them routinely to make sure mold or mildew are not developing.

If you live in a rural area, you might need more than those who live in populated areas. The more people and buildings there are nearby, the less desperate a car wreck or becoming stranded becomes.

My reason for bringing this up is because our minds are active even while we're driving. If you commute to work, your mood and productivity when you arrive at work can be positively or negatively affected by the condition of our vehicle. Like feeling good because we dressed up for an evening, our vehicle can make us glad to be in it or sad to be in it. It doesn't take long to change it.

The front floorboard might be used for transporting an item, but avoid using a space like this for storage.

WHAT ABOUT TRAVEL?

Personal management of space doesn't stop at our office—it follows us wherever we go—even on planes, trains and buses. The more you feel organized you are, the more productive you're likely to be. So, let's take a moment and think about travel. Without trying to delineate short or long-term travel too much, let's just discuss a few basics.

Suitcase Style

Getting the perfect suitcase is fool's errand. Getting a good suitcase just takes some assessment of how you travel. I've earned my share of glory miles in the sky and in rental cars. Because most airlines charge extra for luggage handling in an attempt to show the "lowest fare," and because of experiences with baggage handling that belonged in a horror movie, I have converted to what has come to be called "carry-on" baggage. I'm referring to travel within my own country and not for extended periods (although most people can manage longer trips with the same amount of clothing required on shorter trips by doing laundry during the trip).

Carry-on luggage allows me to handle my own luggage—at least on the larger planes. Smaller planes still require "gate-checking" luggage and having baggage handlers taking them to and from the planeside.

I have one roller bag that fits in most overhead bins and one roller that fits under the seat in front of me. If a is less than a week and only casual-wear, I can pack in a small hand-duffle instead of the larger roller-bag.

Suitcase Packing

By using a system I can pack up from a hotel room in five minutes or less. Everything in the suitcase goes in the same place each time, I can do a quick assessment of what might be missing just because a "spot" in my suitcase is empty. If you just throw things in anywhere, you have no idea what has been collected from the room. For example: I once retrieved and item that I inadvertently pushed behind a lamp just because the suitcase contained an empty spot. Basically, my suitcase told me something was still in the room. This method saved me a trip to the store to replace what I almost left. The result: I saved time!

How many times will you have to make a trip to a local convenience store to replace an item before you realize how much time could be saved if the suitcase were packed using a systematic approach?

Purpose/Use

I travel with a laptop, projector and a plethora of cables and cords. All of these go in one suitcase. All of my personal items go in another. I do not put anything for the classroom in my hotel room suitcase. I do not put anything for the hotel room in the classroom suitcase. This prevents wasted time having to run for something left in the other suitcase.

Cubes

Compartmentalizing items in packable cubes is another way to conserve space and time. These compartments serve to separate types of items from other types. So, socks can be kept together, likewise underwear, toiletries, etc. I have cubes that vary, not only in shape and size, but also in color. This makes identifying what I'm looking for much quicker. There are compartments big enough for shirts and pants. I generally only use these for dress pants and coats. The military version of rolling soft items like clothing works better for me with most items.

Order of use

The last travel personal management item I wish to address is how to pack the suitcase. There are some items you will use every day. There are others that will only be used once on the trip (or until laundered). Daily items should be at the top as you open the suitcase. Items not needed until later should be at the bottom.

There is no point in digging past something every day that you do not need for a couple of days. Think in terms of order of use. Pack accordingly.

There you have it. I have tried to discuss everything from workspace to vehicles to suitcases and how it can be turned to better efficiency. Space can be used to save time or misused to cost you time because of distractions and searches. Remember the "one-in-one-out" rule and bind yourself to it.

I'm not going to go into your home and try to make suggestions. That is an area I do not wish to address. You have the principles, but it is your castle. I have a hunch some changes could save you some time, but I'll leave that to you.

SUMMARY

- How much discipline have you developed for putting things away?

- How would you rate yourself at handling paper the minimum number of times?

- How good would you say your use of space is?

    - In your office?

    - In your vehicle?

    - In your home?

    - In your luggage?

PRIORITIZING OUR LIFE

MAKING TIME MEAN SOMETHING IMPORTANT

What good is good use of time if use of time isn't good (say that 3 times quickly)?

At the end of the day, each person's increased efficiency must be seen to accomplish what is important to them.

We achieve this by developing long range goals. While not technically a personal (time) management technique, no arrangement of time and priorities can be divorced from the long-range plan. After all we need to connect this efficiency (saved time) to a goal or endpoint. The key in developing a long-range goal centers around several factors which include:

- What does and does not belong in your world of time/ priorities?

- Who you are or want to become and what is important to you?

If you fail to answer these questions, you cannot begin to effectively manage your time and priorities. Your decisions and processes become random in nature, taking you places you did not intend.

The first time you try to clarify this set of core beliefs, the task seems daunting. But it need not be. Don't feel like your first attempt must be your last. Make a first attempt. I am a firm believer that actions speak louder than words.

Think of it this way. You are not about to *establish* what you believe, you are simply going to bring out what you already believe. For some of you, this will be a very easy process because your actions are very congruent with what you have convinced yourself you believe. For others, this process will be troubling because it will expose the lack of congruency between your stated beliefs and your actions.

For example, the person who purports to believe in honesty as a guiding principle, but practices deception or outright lying to avoid consequences or an unpleasant situation, is out of congruence. The person says they believe in honesty. They may *think* that they believe in honesty, but their actions say they do not. In other words, their actions are out of congruence with their words.

Still for others, this will be an exploration of uncharted waters.

Before we begin, let me speak to those who want to do this in one sitting and perfectly the from the get-go.

Two words: *ain't happening*. Long-range planning is hard work and usually requires re-thinking and re-working numerous times.

The first time you work through your life-destination and how to get there will be like a rough draft. Set a time limit, say a month later, and take another look and edit your ideas. Then set another time about three months later and do it again. Review about six months and a year out. By the end of five or six edits, you should be getting closer to what you really want out of life. If not, you need to do some serious thinking about whether you want to end up at the end of your life regretting where you wound up.

Let's say you decide to drive across the USA. How would you go about this? The first and obvious thought would be from where to where. You would probably use where you're living as the starting point and pick the point you want to end up. Let's say you're in upstate New York and you wish to go to San Diego, CA. Alright, first determination made. But what about the return trip? I need to know if I will call the trip done at San Diego and get on a plane to fly home.

This would mean I might be driving across country in a rental car. Or am I using the return trip to see different parts of the country? Now I might use my own vehicle. Perhaps I leave a rental car in San Diego and take a ship through the Panama Canal to Florida and rent another car to drive back to New York. These decisions represent the longest goal of this particular idea and are representative of what I will call a *Life Mission Statement*. Where do I want to end up and what's needed to get there?

Next, I need to ask myself what sights along the way are important enough to see, how long will it take to see them, and how much out of my way am I willing to go to include them. For example, if I want to see Mt. Rushmore or the Grand Canyon from the ground, these are not exactly on the most efficient route(s) to San Diego. The Grand Canyon alone will require at least an extra day of driving and, possibly. another day for looking at the Grand Canyon from different places. Do I have enough time and budget to include it? How much will I regret not including it?

Next, I need to divide the trip into shorter segments to determine a reasonable amount of distance to cover each day. This probably includes balancing the total time and cost against the smaller decisions. If I see enough stops to make the trip 10 days, and I had originally wanted to be in San Diego in a week, something has to give. Either I extend the time of the trip or some sights will be left out. Budget might also come into play.

Finally, I need to decide how to document the trip. I could keep a written journal, an audio or video account, or still photos only, or some combination of the above. This should be planned before the trip.

What I'm trying to illustrate here is that our life is like the cross-country trip. Many people just start driving with no arrival point in mind. They stop or not based on unclear points of determination. One day they look up from life in St. Louis and try to tell themselves that St. Louis wasn't so bad, but deep down they are wishing they had gone all the way to San Diego, and now it's too late. They live with what happened because they didn't work out a plan.

Life needs to be treated like a cross-country trip. We determine what we want the final destination to be. Then, we start filling in specific wishes and desires along the way. Then we start doing the practical planning that will facilitate this happening. Of course with a cross-country trip, we also determine when to make the trip based on things like time of year, weather and budgeting.

Except in life, we're already in the car. The longer we wait to make choices, the better the chance we end up someplace that was not on the route.

Let's call the trip to San Diego the *Life Mission Statement*. Let's call sights to see along the road *Goals*. And let's call the practical planning *My Action Plan (M.A.P.)*.

There will be three other parts that we will include as well. We will refer to these as:

(1) *Roles*. These are the categories of our life where there may be separate desires and accomplishments,

(2) *WHaT* (What Happened Today). we will need a daily record of activities and events to compare to the intended goals

(3) *Accountability system*. There needs to be an accountability system so that this long-range work is not forgotten. We need a systematic review that keeps us on course. This is a matter of scheduling review times and actually doing the review.

Okay. Are you ready to dive in? This needs some serious thinking time that is relatively free from interruptions.

LIFE MISSION STATEMENT

The best way to describe a *Life Mission Statement* is to imagine you get to write your own tombstone. What do you want on it? How do you want to be remembered?

Make a stab at writing your epitaph. Don't worry about perfection. You will likely refine this as you make edits in the future. You'll think of better ways to say something. You may realize you have only stated part of what is actually a larger goal. That's why it's important to make a start, but not feel as though this is written in stone and cannot be modified. Paragraph format of approximately 3-5 sentences should be adequate for most individuals. Let's get started.

Take a blank sheet of paper or open a word processing file and write/type "Mission Statement" at the top. This is the term commonly used for a written statement describing your core belief system.

Then ask yourself what you believe to be absolutely true about yourself. Write fairly short, declarative sentences. This is not the time for editing the sound and flow of the words. This is a time to capture the essence of your thoughts. I find mind mapping to be enormously helpful in this exercise.

After making a few statements you believe to be true about yourself, raise the bar just a bit and make a few statements about who you would like to become. This is where you change from what is currently true about yourself into shaping who you want to become.

After you have written several of these declarative statements, put a mark beside any for which you suspect there are incongruences with your current actions.

After you have a good start in writing the short, declarative sentences, decide whether you want to keep these in this format, a bullet format, or turn them into a paragraph format. This is entirely your decision.

I would caution you against turning this into paragraph format too soon. You might consider waiting until you have been through several drafts to avoid unnecessary administrative burden. The perfectionists among us can waste a lot of time on the formatting prematurely.

Take your statements seriously. Build them into the fabric of your being. Some of them are already there. Others need to be cultivated like a garden.

By the way, writing a mission statement and never reviewing it is a waste of time. You must include a systematic and regular review of these statements in order for them to have the effect you would like them to have.

Here are some sentence fragments that might guide you in writing one or more complete sentences for your *Life Mission Statement*.

- Priority of family

- Dedicated employee

- A person of integrity, godly and loving

- Made others feel important

- Seemed to always do the right thing

- Lived life to the fullest

- Honest, yet kind

- Inspired/Brought out best in others

- God, Family, Country

Here is an example of a mission statement:

Spend more face time with the people [I] care about and [do] the things that give [me] the greatest amount of joy in life.[1]

Sometimes we can cover a lot of ground on these by listing character qualities. A few are mentioned above, but there are many others.

---

1   Eat That Frog by Brian Tracy

This is where we pause and ask ourselves what categories (buckets) we might have. Think of them as uniquely separate ideas about what to accomplish. We need to realize that different roles will call for different desired outcomes. If you haven't already done so, think about your life right now and ask how many roles or categories currently make up your life. Examples might include:

- Family

- Spiritual/Church/Synagogue

- Career

- Health/Physical

- Hobby/Hobbies

Most people run out of time and motivation when there are more than six categories. Having more roles probably means not doing justice to at least some of them. After all, there are only 24 hours in a day and seven days in a week.

So, now we can start asking what stops along the journey will each *role* play and require. Keep these rather philosophical at this point. We're not ready to get too specific yet. I recommend at least one stop for each role, but not more than two or three.

Perhaps under the role of family you might say, "I want my marriage to be thriving" or "I want to raise children who are independent and productive." Under "career" you might say, "I want to own a business that supports my needs and requires less than four hours of my time each week to accomplish it."

For the role of health, you might have a goal of weighing a certain amount, re-sculpting your shape, finishing a marathon, or getting a certain score in golf.

Now that we have our journey divided into buckets, let's start thinking about what's important along the way. These have come to be called a *bucket list* and refer to the things we would like to accomplish before we kick the bucket. Because we often have an expectation of living a long life, many wait until later years. It is much better to begin working on such a list at a younger age.

Let's break this journey down by thinking about where you would like to be in 10 years, five years and next year for each bucket.

If, under the hobby bucket, you want to sail around the world, what would it take to do that? Buy or lease a sailboat? Take sailing lessons?

If this bucket list item requires you having a year or five years or more to accomplish, how many years will it take to make it happen? I know a man that quit his job, sold his house and almost everything he owned, and spent five years sailing around the world with his wife. When he got back, they were both young enough to pick up a new job/career and go on with life. Some of us would need to plan to retire to sail around the world, betting on health and finances to cooperate. You cannot complete this section for each bucket unless you are willing to dream big and dispense with false modesty.

Do you want to skydive, become a pilot, walk a runway in a fashion show, or just build that rustic mountain cabin with enough acreage to live quietly? Perhaps you would like to visit each continent, take a photo safari, or write a novel.

I'm thinking about the movie/documentary called *Band of Brothers*. Army Major Richard Winters of Easy Company had one great desire after WWII: to find a quiet place to live out his life far from war.

No one knows your deepest desires, but they are often things that might bring ridicule from those who are skeptical that such things can happen with a plan.

Most of these dreams will bring ridicule from those who cannot discipline themselves to make dreams happen. Ignore those folks. Dream big. It is better to dream big and come close than not dream at all and hit a target with no *Wow Factor*.

To accomplish these dreams, it is sometimes better to work backwards, while at other times, require you to work from the 1 year, to the 5-year to the 10-year goals.

Although apps are available (check out Brian Tracey's goal setting app in the app store). I really prefer to start with paper. This allows for keeping everything visible while scribbling, scratching out and rewriting. I would recommend making several copies that might look like the following diagram.

Role: _____.

Life Mission Statement: _____

_____

_____

_____

_____

10 Year Goal: _____

5 Year Goal: _____

1 Year Goal: _____

Immediate Actions: _____

_____

_____

_____

_____

_____

Let each page have exactly the same *Life Mission Statement* as you currently have it. This helps keep you on course and allows you to devise ideas that have cohesiveness. Besides, the more you write/type something, the more you will own it.

Once you have accomplished this, it is a matter of having these where they can be reviewed weekly before making out a weekly action plan. At least one of these goals should be included in some part of each week's *M.A.P. (My Action Plan)*.

Often work dictates many of our actions, but if we do not forcibly work toward our own goals they are not likely to happen. I have referred to a weekly planning session because it helps us steer a steadier course based on priorities rather than being sucked into a reactionary lifestyle that merely puts out fires. Those who plan daily often fall victim to being the bomb-squad for disarming the latest bomb threatening someone or something at work.

Daily adjustments can be made as the *WHaT* shows we didn't precisely fulfill the plan as we envisioned it at the beginning of the week. However, we are more likely to achieve the more important items if we take a little longer look at these items daily.

The only thing left to discuss now is keeping a record of each day so it can be reviewed before each week's planning session. This is what I have come to call a *WHaT (What Happened Today)*. Without doing an *A.A.R. (After Action Report)*, we do not have the ability to make proper course corrections. This is when we begin the inevitable drift that happens with the press of life.

I cannot stress enough that if anyone fails to follow through on this chapter, it is almost always because the weekly review of the previous week and the long-range goals are abandoned. Vigilance will always see more finishes than great starts.

Think hard.

Dream Big.

Align steps.

Happy Life.

CHAPTER APPLICATION

1. Schedule an uninterruptible time

2. Take a sheet of paper or sit at a mind map program

3. Take a stab at a Life Mission Statement

4. Start imagining who you would like to be. Let your thoughts run in any direction.

    a. What would your spiritual life consist of?

    b. What message would you want your physical appearance to send? What physical shape would be appropriate?

    c. How much of an intellectual an image would you want to project?

    d. etc.

5. Think through the roles in your life (existing or desired)

6. Ask what 10 years would need to look like (spiritual, physical, mental)

7. Ask what 5 years would need to look like (spiritual, physical, mental)

8. Ask where you would need to be next year

9. Ask what specific steps would be required. e.g.

    a. Do you need to enroll in any classes?

        i. Religious?

        ii. Adult education at a local college or university?

        iii. Ballet or exercise?

    b. Do you need to change your morning or evening (or both) routine to include spiritual meditation, self-help study, or exercise?

    c. Etc.

10. Put all of this where it can be reviewed on a weekly basis before weekly planning.

11. Make sure something off the list makes each week's schedule.

SUMMARY

Do you have a map and a plan for your life, or are you just "rolling" without a life goal?

CONCLUSION

Well, that about raps it up. This is a journey more than a destination. Little changes here and there will do more to increase efficiency in the management of your personal life and help you get more done and free up more time for whatever it is that makes you want more free time.

After all, your time is valuable and the only investment from which you cannot recover from poor choices.

Maintaining the Momentum

The biggest problem with time management books is that we get motivated while we're reading the book, but do not follow through on the idea to make the long-term changes required. I would like to use the final part of this book to address.

Follow-through. What would be the equivalent of follow-through in this case?

I suggest it is keeping a log of activities to compare with the plan of activities. (See *WHaT* mentioned in chapter 7.) This is not something that can be done constantly, but rather just occasionally. Keeping a paper form to the side of your work area and logging every 15 minutes what the last 15 minutes actually contained is an eye-opening revelation to most of us. There are also a number of apps that can track our activity (See a*TimeLogger* in the app store). This would greatly slow down productivity if kept every day. Constantly monitoring our day minute by minute isn't necessary.

Typically, right after reading a book like this the motivation will allow us to keep that detailed log for a couple of weeks. That should give you a good read on what your time is actually being used to accomplish. Then change the 15-minute log into an hourly, semi-daily, or even daily record.

If you skip the *WHaT*, momentum is lost and then you will return to the old habits that frustrated you enough to read this book in the first place.

So here is a possible plan. Start with a 15-minute log for 2 weeks. Then go to a twice a day WHaT. About six months from now, do a 30-minute log for 3 consecutive days (or a week). At least once a year, do something more detailed than the *WHaT* for at least 3 consecutive days. This will serve to keep you on course much like firing a retro on a rocket for minor course corrections. Be somewhat brutal on comparing what you *did* do with what you *planned* to do. Make changes when necessary.

You keep track of weight, calories, exercise, and receipts. Why not keep track of time?

One final tip might be to take a reading course. If you're like most people, a certain amount of required reading is a part of your life. Increasing your reading speed and comprehension can be a real productivity and efficiency boost. Even if you only read for fun.

Enjoy the Journey.

Morning Routine
Bedside Stretch
Bathroom/Wash Face & Hands
Drink Water
Check/Adjust Thermostat
Inspirational Reading/Meditate
Exercise
Coffee/Tea
Check Social Media (time limit)
Check Email*
Shower
Personal Grooming/Hygiene
Take Vitamins/Medication
Eat/Jumpstart Metabolism
Family Routine
Look Over/Adjust Today's Plan
Gather Needed Items
* Dont get thrown off your plan!

	Evening Routine
	Tweak Tomorrow's Schedule
	Check/Adjust Thermostat
	Drink Water
	Brush/floss teeth
	Dress for sleep,
	Turn the covers back
	Drink water
	Take medication(s)
	Journal
	Focus on something inspirational
	Clear any negative emotions
	Verbalize love to family members
	Tuck children in/read to them
	Look over tomorrow's plan
	Adjust thermostat
	Set alarm
	Dress for Bed
	Read/Relax

Weekly Routine

	Filing
	Write Weekly Reports
	Vacuum/Straighten Office
	Change Waiting Area Reading Material
	Water Plants
	Feed Fish
	Run Computer Updates
	Shut Down Computer
	Take Something Home to be Cleaned
	Laundry
	Dusting/Vacuuming
	Mowing/Gardening
	Banking
	Grocery Shopping (Use List)
	Cooking for Upcoming Week (Freeze)
	Workout

Quarterly Routine

	Deep Clean
	Financial Reports/Tax Filings
	Change Seasonal Decorations
	Service Vehicles

Semiannual Routine
Replace Smoke Detector Batteries
Defrost Freezer
Change HVAC Filters
Clean/Organize Shed/Garage/Storage
Clean Gutters
Inspect Roof/Driveway
Change Screens/Storm Windows
Prepare RV for Coming Months
Put Flag Out/Take Flag In

Annual Routine
File Taxes
Schedule Vacation
Plan Family Holidays/Travel
Decide on Major Purchases
Make Changes to Healthcare
Major Maintenance (House Painting, etc.)

Work
Attaché/Briefcase/Purse/Duffle/Backpack
Today's Files/Docs
Pen(s)
Wallet/Coins/Driver's License
Calendar/Appt./To-Do
Weather appropriate clothing/glasses
Shine Shoes
House Keys
Vehicle Keys
Office Keys
Hard Hat
Tool Bag

The next few checklists have to do with some type of travel. I would like to offer a few tips gleaned along the way.

✓ Travelers' proverb: "Take half of what you think you need—and twice as much cash."

✓ Travel with clothing commonly referred to as "mix and match." i.e. uppers can be used with more than one lower and vice versa. Use as much "wrinkle free" and easy drying as possible.

✓ First in—last out. Put the items that will be used first on top.

✓ Determine if "rolling" or "cubes" are better for you. Packable cubes are better in some instances. Rolling clothing is better in other instances. To some extent this has to do with the type of luggage used.

✓ Use all available space. Pack socks and underwear inside shoes, etc. Leave no empty space.

✓ Leave room for purchases on trip. Try packing a smaller suitcase and putting it inside a larger suitcase. On the return trip the larger suitcase is used for souvenirs and gifts. Or pack a soft duffle inside a suitcase.

Flight Comfort
Motion Aids
Ear Plugs
Chewing Gum
Sleep Mask
Neck Pillow
Snacks
Phone and/or Tablet (with chargers)
Headphones/Earphones
Movie Downloads
Reading (Paper, eBooks)
Audio Books (with earphones)
Music Playlists

Documents

	Tickets/Boarding Passes
	Visas
	Passport (copy in separate location)
	Credit Card(s) (w/ emer. contact info)
	Driver's License
	Proof of Vehicle Insurance
	Medical Insurance Card
	List of Meds/Schedule
	Travel Guides
	Travel Journal
	Itinerary (copy with trusted person)
	Membership Cards
	Wallet
	Cash (in Money Belt or Neck Pouch)

Luggage

	Large Suitcase
	Small Suitcase
	Carry-On Suitcase
	Backpack/Briefcase/Purse
	Document Pouch on Neck Strap
	Luggage Tags
	Internal Luggage ID's
	Key Container
	TSA Approved Toiletry Bag

Laundry

	Plastic Bags
	Sewing Kit
	Travel Iron/Steamer
	Dry Bar Laundry Soap

Electronics

	Phone/Charger
	Tablet/Charger
	Laptop/Power Cord
	Camera/Power Cord
	Universal Voltage Adapter
	Batteries
	Travel Alarm
	Flashlight
	Memory Storage for Pictures

First Aid Kit

	Pain Reliever
	Antiseptic
	Bandages
	Sunscreen
	Insect Repellant
	Sunburn Lotion
	Allergy Medication
	Anti-diarrhea
	Laxative

	Miscellaneous
	Watch
	Jewelry
	Umbrella
	Binoculars
	Glasses/Case
	Contacts/Case/Solution
	Sunglasses
	Lint Remover
	Stain Remover
	Filtered Water Bottle
	Plastic Bag(s) for dirty laundry/shoes
	Sleepwear (pajamas/gown/slippers)

	Dress Clothing
	Suit(s)/Dresses/Skirts
	Dress Shirt(s)/Blouses
	Ties
	Slack(s)
	Underwear
	Bras
	Dress Socks/Hosiery
	Dress Shoes
	Dress Belt

Casual Clothing

	Casual Collared Shirt
	T-Shirts (Long/Short Sleeve)
	Cargo Pants
	Casual Slacks
	Shorts
	Sweatshirt(s)
	Sweatpants
	Denims
	Workout Clothes
	Athletic Socks
	Athletic Shoes
	Hiking Boots
	Boot Socks

Outdoor Clothing

	Overcoat/Raincoat
	Lightweight/Warm Weather Clothing
	Medium Weight/Cool Weather Clothing
	Heavy Weight/Cold Weather Clothing
	Head Cover
	Face Cover
	Ear Cover
	Hands Cover
	Scarf
	Moisture Wicking Upper
	Moisture Wicking Torso
	Moisture Wicking Socks
	Water Resistant Shoes/Boots

Outdoor Clothing

	Toiletry Bag/Case
	Toothbrush
	Toothpaste
	Mouthwash
	Floss
	Hair Products
	Hair Accessories
	Cologne/Perfume
	Hairbrush/Comb
	Deodorant
	Shampoo
	Conditioner
	Wipes
	Q-Tips
	Razor
	Shaving Cream
	After Shave
	Lip Balm
	Face Lotion
	Hand Lotion
	Body Lotion
	Tissue
	Cotton Balls/Swabs
	Tweezers
	Nail Clippers
	Gauze
	Makeup
	Makeup Remover
	Feminine Hygiene

Outdoor Clothing
Nail Clippers
Nail File/Board
Nail Polish & Remover
Hand Sanitizer
Vitamins

Beach Clothing
Swimsuit
Over Swimsuit Cover Up
Deck Shoes/Flip-Flops
A-shirt/Sleeveless Shirt/Tank Top
Waterproof Beach Bag

Grocery Shopping
Instead of reinventing the wheel, I would like to submit this URL from "grocerylists.org" as a great grocery checklist. http://www.grocerylists.org/wp-content/uploads/2013/01/grocerylistsDOTorg_Deluxe_v3_3.pdf

The point of all these lists is to get in the habit of using lists instead of memory. Memory is faulty. Lists help insure nothing is missed or forgotten.

Start making and using your own checklists for anything and everything. E.g. I have a checklist beside the stove for when I have to cook. This keeps me from having to keep repeating lists I need frequently.

101 TIME MANAGEMENT TIPS

1. **Manage Yourself:** We manage ourselves, not time. Time is fixed. Personal management is about self-discipline.

2. **Invest Wisely:** Time is the only investment for which there is no recovery.

3. **Control:** Start with what you can control. Accept what you can't control.

4. **Write Everything Down:** Memory is the worst system you can use. Never trust your memory when it comes to tasks and appointments.

5. **Write It Down Now:** The sooner you capture something the less stress you experience.

6. **Write Everything in One Place:** Recording in multiple places means having to remember where. Writing in one place relieves the stress of remembering where you wrote it.

7. **Write Only Where Info Is Convenient and Accessible:** A system that is not convenient or accessible ensures you will return to using your memory.

8. **Tweak an Existing System:** Sometimes tweaking the system you already have is better than trying to reinvent the wheel.

9. **Scrap Failing Systems:** If your system is failing, scrap it and do something else.

10. **Avoid Insanity:** Doing the same thing over and over will not change the results.

11. **Avoid Multitasking:** Do not attempt it. Switching between tasks is much slower. Concentrate on current task. Only after completion of first task should you move to the next task.

12. **Sleep:** Get enough sleep

13. **Calendar:** Use only one calendar to schedule all appointments, meetings, and tasks requirements. Use no more than 6 color codes on your calendar.

14. **Do Most Important Things First:** Don't let trivial tasks eat time needed for your priorities.

15. **Don't Avoid The Hardest Tasks:** Tackle these tasks when your energy is the highest.

16. **Don't Waste Time Dreading Tasks. Do Them:** Getting ugly tasks done improves the outlook on the rest of the day. Avoid dreading a task longer than it takes to do it.

17. **Focus:** Distractions slow efficiency. Focus on the task at hand. Do not allow yourself to be distracted.

18. **Consider 80/20 Rule:** 80% of your time on is often on 20% of what you need to do. Work on the 20% that gives you the biggest result.

19. **Divide Difficult/Long Projects:** Divide long projects into manageable parts. The longest project is accomplished by focusing on the next step, not the next 10 steps.

20. **Make a MAP:** My Action Plan is a personal organizational plan that navigates you through your work.

21. **Start Early:** Coming out of the starting blocks at the beginning of the day/shift reduces wasted time.

22. **Compare:** Make sure your effort resembles your plan. Make sure you completed everything, dropped it as no longer relevant, or added it to this week's tasks.

23. **Think Forward:** What would take less time to accomplish with better planning? Look out a week, a month, a quarter, and a year.

24. **Read Effectively:** Learn how to scan through documents, rather than trying to read every word.

25. **Take a Speed Reading Course:** The better you read, the faster you read, the more you accomplish – usually needing to ask fewer question of others.

26. **Reduce Meetings:** Only schedule meetings when necessary.

27. **Touch Paper Only Once:** Use the "one-touch" rule on paper handling.

28. **Ensure You Have Enough Time Before Picking Something Up:** Don't touch paper or mail unless you are prepared to take action (complete it or schedule it).

29. **Prepare to Deal with Paper:** Have your to-do list at hand (MAP) for items needing action at a later time.

30. **Throw Away What Is Not Valuable:** Hesitation means dubious value.

31. **Open Mail Over Trash:** Never open mail unless standing over/near a trashcan and ensure you have time to deal with important mail NOW or record it in you MAP.

32. **Use Email/Text:** Consider if email/text will be more efficient, especially if you need a paper trail/record.

33. **Stay Close to Goals:** What do you want to achieve for the day, week, month, year? Make 3 goals for each area and monitor progress.

34. **Separate Important from Urgent:** Complete tasks by importance rather than urgency. Learn the Eisenhower diagram for separating important and urgent.

35. **Control Entertainment:** Monitor the amount of time you spend on things like talking to coworkers, TV, gaming, etc. Recreation (re—creation) is good. Wasted time is not.

36. **Put Entertainment on a Plan:** Plan TV/Movie viewing for the week ahead. Set a recording device to gain control over when and how long to watch. Watch later when it fits your schedule.

37. **Stay Up Late**: If you have failed to meet a goal or complete a task, stay up late and get it done! This serves two purposes: 1). You get it done. 2). You teach yourself not to procrastinate or allow something to interfere with your plan.

38. **De-clutter Work Space:** Make sure your work space is organized, clean, and neat. People can tell a lot about your organization and time management skills by looking at your work space.

39. **Organize Religiously:** You must be organized! Chaos will reduce your efficiency.

40. **Set Task Time Limits:** Assign a time limit for each task.

41. **Respect Deadlines:** If a deadline is not important, don't set it. If a deadline is important, respect it.

42. **List Tasks Under Project Headings:** Ensure you maintain a list of projects broken into the tasks it will take to complete them.

43. **Make Secondary Deadlines:** If you do not meet a deadline consider renegotiating the deadline with the appropriate individual.

44. **Be Where Your Feet Are:** Always think about the task at hand. Do not allow yourself to become distracted by the other contexts of your life or tasks that cannot be accomplished where you are.

45. **Schedule Breaks:** Standing, walking, etc. increases concentration. Try stretching 5 minutes out of each half hour. This is also a great time to handle minor interruptions and prepare for the next task.

46. **Take Notes:** When in a meeting or on the telephone take notes.

47. **Plan Your Work / Work Your Plan:** Plan as far ahead as is practical. The further you plan, the more likely you'll accomplish the important rather than the urgent.

48. **Schedule Weekly Planning:** Schedule 30 minutes at the same time each week to plan the upcoming week. Weekly planning sticks closer to priorities. Daily planning is pressured by urgent, but not necessarily important.

49. **Use Weekends Wisely:** If you choose to use your weekends, only use a small part. Schedule the time. Complete the tasks you need to complete and only the tasks you need to complete. Then rest!

50. **Use Colored Folders for Categories:** Use different colored folders for different types of actions. For example; blue could represent awards, black-evaluations, green-administrative actions, RED-Urgent must be completed before you go home.

51. **Use Colors in an Organizer / Lists / Calendar Apps:** Use different colors to differentiate between up to six different roles in your life.

52. **Try Colored Sticky Notes:** Sometimes colored sticky notes can be used instead of colored folders. Sometimes both can be used for more detailed organization.

53. **Know the End Goal:** Know what your end product is supposed to look like. Never start a project until you have a picture of the finished project.

54. **Plan for Down Time:** Always have something to read or work on for when you get unexpected down time, such as being put on hold or waiting for an appointment.

55. **Exile Yourself When Important Deadlines Are Looming:** When tasks are critical close the door, lock yourself in and place a "DO NOT DISTURB" sign on your door.

56. **Consider Pairing Up:** Where it makes since pair up with a coworker or team member.

57. **Delegate:** If a task is not of a private nature or something that you must do, delegate it.

58. **Review:** Review your list often. Writing something down does no good if you do not review it.

59. **Plan a Start/Stop Time:** Schedule a start and stop time for every task and every meeting over which you have control.

60. **Don't Procrastinate:** Do it NOW! Do not procrastinate. Procrastination kills.

61. **Batch:** Put like tasks together. Grouping similar tasks is more efficient.

62. **Purge Unnecessary Tasks:** Remove any unnecessary tasks from your list.

63. **Do Not Overcommit:** Do not over commit yourself! Learn how to "say, NO!"

64. **Put Routines into Checklists:** Develop routines for recurring activities. Start with checklists and modify them as you go. Don't try to remember.

65. **Stick to The Plan:** Don't let distractions such as email and surprise requests cause you to deviate from your plan.

66. **Organize Workspace:** Use the "Area A, B, C, D" method.

67. **Send Written Agendas/Materials:** Meeting Agendas or materials should be in written form and sent with enough time for the attendees to prepare.

68. **Schedule Org/Cleaning Time:** Make at least a weekly routine checklist for cleaning/filing/organization.

69. **Put Everything Away:** Do not set things down to put away later. Put it all the way away now.

70. **Schedule Hard Appointments:** Calendar the appointments you cannot control. What is left is time you can control.

71. **Turn Tasks into Soft Appointments:** Tasks require time. Time is finite, so the calendar ultimately determines how much gets done.

72. **Calendar Deadlines:** Meeting deadlines requires scheduling work ahead of deadlines.

73. **Prioritize:** When faced with too many important tasks, ask a supervisor which ones require priority attention.

74. **Ignore or Eliminate Distractions:** Phones, social media, email, chatty coworkers may be urgent, but that does not mean they are

more important than what you are doing. If important, deal with distractions during breaks.

75. **Learn and Use the Pomodoro Method:** Learn to block time into concentrated segments to prevent distractions from slowing you down.

76. **Adjust Daily:** Rethink priorities daily. Keep urgencies from crowding out priorities.

77. **Schedule Time for Disasters:** Unexpected emergencies do happen. Deal with them. If no disasters happen, ask what additional items can be achieved.

78. **Beware Email:** Consider email a temptation to work on what someone else wants instead of what is important to you — unless your job description calls for responding instantly to email.

79. **Turn Off All Alerts:** Only allow alerts you control and only when they are helpful for staying on task/schedule.

80. **Always Use Triggers:** Learn to use "triggers" to put an important item in front of you at the right time without having to carry it in your memory.

81. **Sync Work with Circadian Rhythms:** Learn your "circadian rhythms" to use your best energy on most important tasks.

82. **Dream:** Plan regular times for thinking ahead and dreaming about what could happen.

83. **Capture Dreams:** Create a place where ideas not ready for action can be captured. Capture your dreams there awaiting a time for action.

84. **Consider Themes for Days:** e.g. Monday for Meetings, Tuesday for Menial Tasks, Wednesday for Writing Reports, etc.

85. **Use Mind Mapping:** Learn to mind mapping on all creative thinking. Practice mind mapping as often as is practical.

86. **Control Social Media Time:** Ruthlessly limit social media time that does not directly contribute to productivity.

87. **Remove Unhelpful Alerts:** Anything that pulls you from your plan/schedule needs to be turned off. This does not apply to instant availability to a superior if your job descriptions requires it.

88. **Publish When You Are Available:** Consider using an signature line in your email that tells others when you will respond. Only respond on your schedule. Put an office hours sign outside your office.

89. **Throw Away:** Eliminate anything you're not SURE you can use in the future.

90. **Remove Clutter from Vehicles Routinely:** Schedule going through seats, trunk, console and/or glovebox.

91. **Pack with a Purpose:** Pack with "first in last use, last in first use" rule.

92. **Utilize Outer Luggage Compartments:** Anything you might need during travel should be easily accessible without having to open and disturb the main compartment.

93. **Utilize All Luggage Space:** Don't waste space with empty air. Use insides of shoes, etc.

94. **Roll It or Cube It:** Decide if rolling or using cubes to compartmentalize is best.

95. **Pack Lightly:** Except for emergency/survival items, pack only what you KNOW you will need.

96. **Pack Smartly:** The travelers' rule is "pack half of what you think you'll need and twice as much cash."

97. **Make Duplicates of Important Documents:** Put copies in separate places to avoid losing both.

98. **Pack Everything in the Same Place:** When traveling know what belongs where in your luggage to prevent forgetting items.

99. **Pack for the Return:** Will you need extra space coming back? Consider packing with smaller luggage inside a larger one to allow extra space on return.

100. **Be Prepared to Record:** Always keep pen and paper handy for those unexpected thoughts, and actions. Transfer them to your one capture point as soon as is practical.

101. **Journal religiously:** Finish each day with a record of what you did and your thoughts about your accomplishments.